Beppi

A LIFE IN THREE COURSES

BEPPI POLESE
WITH JOHN NEWTON

PIER
9

MENU

PRIMI

CHAPTER ONE

AN EDUCATION IN EATING

THE TIMES
1925

A SPEECH BY MUSSOLINI ON 3 JANUARY 1925 WAS SEEN
BY HISTORIANS AS THE BEGINNING OF THE END OF ITALY'S
PARLIAMENTARY MOVEMENT. THE DEPRESSION WAS HAVING
A DRASTIC EFFECT ON ITALY'S ECONOMY. UNEMPLOYMENT
WAS RISING DRAMATICALLY. MUSSOLINI ATTEMPTED TO FIGHT
BACK BY NATIONALISING BANKRUPT BUSINESSES AND BY
MAKING ITALY SELF-SUFFICIENT IN GRAIN AND AGRICULTURAL
PRODUCTION. THE SO-CALLED BATTLES FOR GRAIN AND LAND.
THE FIRST OF THE AUTOSTRADAS WERE BUILT USING THE
UNEMPLOYED AS LABOUR. IN 1934 ITALY HOSTED AND WON
THE WORLD CUP.

A curious phenomenon at the time was *The Futurist Cookbook*, published
in 1932. More of a political manifesto and an elaborate Dadaist joke than a
manual for cooking, it was a vehicle for the self-aggrandisement of the leader
of the Futurists, Filippo Tommaso Marinetti, whose most controversial move was
an attempt to ban pasta, which he called 'an absurd Italian gastronomic religion'
and blamed for the 'sluggishness' of Italians. Marinetti's movement, while
affording brief amusement and indignation, failed utterly.

In 1925, Scottish inventor John Logie Baird succeeded in making the first
television transmission of human features. In 1926, he beamed a signal across
the Atlantic and transmitted colour images. (In 1958, Australian television star
Graham Kennedy appropriated Baird's middle name for the industry's awards,
henceforth known as the Logies.)

By 1935, the clouds of war were gathering. Mussolini invaded Ethiopia and Hitler repudiated the 1919 Treaty of Versailles, which specifically forbade Germany from operating weapons of aggression and reduced her army to 100,000. The League of Nations imposed economic sanctions on Italy. By 1936, the Spanish Civil War was raging. In 1938, Italy again won the World Cup—Mussolini did not fare so well. In April 1939, Italy annexed Albania, and in September Hitler invaded Poland. The following year, Italy occupied British Somaliland and attacked British Egypt from Libya, and Greece from Albania. Their troops were pushed back into Libya by the British and Albania by the Greeks.

In 1940, Winston Churchill became prime minister of Britain. Hitler invaded Denmark, the Netherlands, Belgium, France and Luxembourg.

Back from the promised land …
empty-handed

Beppi Polese's earliest memory is playing with pebbles outside an *osteria* (inn), on the day his father Antonio returned from an attempt to make his fortune in Australia. The year was 1931.

Beppi was six, the youngest of five children born to Antonio and Caterina Polese. The eldest being Teresina, born in 1915, then Anna born in 1919, a brother Luigi, or Gigi, in 1921, another sister, Rosa, in 1923 (who died in Ferrara in 1962), and then Beppi in 1925. Antonio was often away, looking for work, and 'every time he came home', Beppi said, 'there'd be another child'.

That day, his mother had loaded four of the five children (Teresina was working in Milan at the time) onto a cart pulled by a donkey, and driven 10 kilometres from their village, San Giovanni di Polcenigo, to the railway station at Sacile—about 100 kilometres from Venice in the mountainous Friuli region of north-east Italy. On the way back they stopped at an *osteria* for lunch. It was the first time any of the children had eaten away from home.

So the two most influential ideas of Beppi's life—that Australia might be a land of opportunity and that people will pay to be served a meal—were embedded in his mind on the same day. It was to be another eight years before his next encounter with the world of hospitality, and another eighteen before Australia again became the subject of serious consideration. But the seeds were planted on that day in the summer of 1931.

Did they serve good food at the *osteria*? 'I have no idea', says Beppi seventy-five years later. 'I imagine mum and dad ate pasta. I don't think I ate anything. I just remember the pebbles.'

Over the following weeks, as life settled back into routine for the Polese family, Beppi heard about his father's experiences as a stranger in a strange land—tales that seemed as exotic as the adventures of Marco Polo, a boy from the same neighbourhood who famously set off centuries earlier in search of fortune and found wonders beyond imagination. This was not the first time Antonio had left home in search of work—he had been to Belgium, Germany and other parts of Italy—but it was the furthest he had travelled.

Beppi remembers a photo of Antonio on the unfinished span of a massive bridge being built across a harbour in a city called Sydney, a photo that had been taken by a relative living in Sydney. When he first saw this photo as a child, the words 'harbour' and 'city' had no meaning for him.

Antonio Polese had worked as a coal miner in Belgium and France in his teenage years, then turned to farming after his first child was born in 1915. But the land he owned yielded barely enough to feed the family, he had borrowed money to build the house they lived in, and there was very little work to be found in Italy at that time.

In 1929, when he saw a poster at the Town Hall in Polcenigo (the commercial centre for the area) showing a far-off land called Australia, which was looking for labourers, he thought a year in a new country might earn him enough to lift his family above the poverty line and offer his children some alternatives to subsistence farming. He borrowed the money to make the trip, but by the time the ship had carried him 16,000 kilometres to the other end of the earth, Australia was deep in economic depression and manual workers were no longer needed.

A few days after settling into a boarding house in East Sydney—just two streets from the spot where his son would later run the city's most fashionable restaurant—Antonio was robbed of the few pounds he had brought with him as emergency money. But he was saved by the bureaucracy. Beppi explains:

> There was no work in the city, so the Immigration Department sent him out to the country, to clear spinifex on a farm outside Quirindi [near Tamworth in north-western New South Wales]. He thought at least he would have enough to eat, because in the country they can always kill a sheep. One of his jobs was to go to the post box to pick up the mail. They said, 'Take the horse'. He said, 'But I can't ride a horse'. So they said, 'Well, you have to walk'. It was more than 16 kilometres. He did it twice on foot, and then, with great persistence, he learnt to ride.

In the end he couldn't see any hope to achieve anything. He was earning £1 a week, which he sent to Caterina to pay back the two loans—one to build the house and the other for the return fare to Australia—and after two years, he decided to come back to Italy. He got off the ship in Genoa and caught a train to Milan, where my sister Teresina was working as a maid. He was destitute and ashamed to go straight home, because he didn't have decent clothing—he was wearing the same clothing he had when he'd left Italy two years before. My sister borrowed money and went to a department store called Rinascente and bought clothing for him. And so he looked presentable when we met him in Sacile.

Antonio Polese did bring back one thing of value—a contact. In Sydney, he had tracked down a distant cousin of Caterina's, Toni de Fort, and they had become friends (it was de Fort who took the picture of Beppi's father on the unfinished Harbour Bridge). The name proved essential to Beppi when he made his own decision to try his luck in Australia twenty-two years later.

Antonio reported that Toni de Fort worked at a bakery in Sydney that made bread and Sargents Pies. The meat pie, a staple in Australia's diet at the time, was another mystifying concept to the Polese children. For them, the staff of life was a coarse powder ground from corn.

The daily polenta.
Family food rituals

Our day started with polenta—a variation called *pestariei*, like porridge, and made with fresh milk—and usually finished with polenta. My mother would get up before 6 am and light the fire in the kitchen. All our cooking was done at a big open fireplace we called the *fogolar*—which in English would be the hearth—and we ate at the tables around it. There was no oven, no stove, just the fire, a steel grill and various pots and pans to hang over it. She would put the water on to boil in a pot hanging from a chain, and make the *pestariei*.

I would wake up about at 6 am and get the hay to feed the cows. Then my father would milk the cows and we would have the fresh milk for caffe latte. This wasn't made with coffee beans, but with *orzo* (barley) that was roasted in a round metal ball that sat in the fire. You grind the blackened barley and boil it up in a pot over the fire, and it's ready when the froth on the top goes flat.

My mother would skim the cream off the previous day's milk, and put the cream in a wide-necked bottle with a cork. It was my job to shake it up and down until it solidified into butter. We would take the rest of the milk to the *latteria sociale* (cooperative dairy), and at the end of the month they would give us ricotta, butter and cheese according to the quantity of milk we provided during the month.

For lunch we would have soup, often with beans, cabbage, tomato, onion and celery, and some cold polenta with cheese. In my area, Friuli, there are about forty different types of soup, depending on the vegetables that are around at different times of year. What was eaten also depended on what each family grew and what wild vegetables were available—radicchio, botonera, gallinella and scropettina—some of these are dialect names for the wild greens.

For dinner it was polenta again, and my (paternal) grandfather Luigi was in charge of stirring it. We didn't have watches, but he had worked out that it would be perfect if you stirred it for the time it takes to say seven rosaries—about 40 minutes, I suppose, but it seemed longer. We'd be sitting around the *fogolar*, watching grandfather mumbling to himself with the rosary beads, mixing the polenta, and asking our mother, 'When will he be finished? We're hungry!'

Finally, the polenta would start to come away from the sides of the copper pot, and it would be ready to eat with cheese, or with sausages and cabbage, or with fried pancetta and salami, or mushrooms, and a big salad of wild greens and other vegetables from the garden. When the salami and pancetta were cooked, my mother would remove them and my father would put vinegar in the pan, mix it in and pour this oily substance and vinegar dressing over the salad—we couldn't afford olive oil.

My grandfather Luigi lived in our house for a while. When his wife died, he went to live with my aunt, Anna Maria Favret, and her family in the house behind ours. But he wasn't happy there; he claimed my cousin used to pinch money from him—taking it from his pocket while he was asleep. He asked my mother if he could come and live with us. My mother reluctantly agreed—because my father was away she decided that he could help with some chores. He wasn't any trouble. He would sit in front of the house, have some lunch, have a siesta. I was ten or eleven when he was there. He used to sleep in a room with my brother and me. He died when I was in Germany in 1944. He was ninety-six.

On Fridays, when the church said we could not eat meat, my mother would sometimes bake salted herrings by the fire on a kind of heavy paper made from wheat stalks. The paper would collect the salty juices and we would dab pieces of polenta on it to collect every last smear of salted herring—it was delicious. Very rarely she would get baby sardines or soft-shell crabs, called 'moeche' in Venetian dialect or 'masonet' in the dialect of Friuli, from a man who came up from Sacile with a box behind his bicycle.

Today, when Beppi thinks back on the time and place of his early childhood, it seems to him almost as if it were someone else's life and circumstances.

At night, sometimes I can't sleep, and I think about my past—my village, the life we had—it's impossible to realise the hard times. I was ten years old before my mother could buy me a second-hand pair of shoes. But we accepted our situation. We didn't know any better, and hadn't been anywhere different. We managed as best as we could and were happy when we had enough food.

It is hard for us to imagine the level of poverty back then, even harder when we look closely at the village and the house that Beppi and his family grew up in. It appears, from this end of his story, to be an idyllic environment, the fulfilment of our modern-day dreams of rustic Italian life.

The village of San Giovanni di Polcenigo is situated on the Friuli-Venezia Giulia (the entire region) side of the border with Veneto, at the foot of the

Left: Beppi's family, from left, Gigi, Mama Caterina, Beppi, Teresina, Papa Antonio, Rosa and Anna.

Alps (with the Dolomites behind) on the edge of the Veneto Padana Plain. Behind it is a series of rolling forest-covered hills leading up to four mountains, the tallest being Cimon del Cavallo at around 2251 metres, about 100 kilometres from Venice.

Polcenigo is the communal centre for the surrounding villages, which includes—besides San Giovanni—Coltura, Mezzomonte, and Gorgazzo, all of which were higher in the hills than San Giovanni. The population of San Giovanni today at around 1000 would have been about the same when Beppi was a boy. The fourteenth-century church of San Giovanni Batista dominated the village, and the piazza in front of that church was the main public space. Around it were an *osteria*, the local bar and café, the dairy cooperative (where young Beppi would take the milk) and the school close by.

The Polese house, like most in the village, had a red-tiled roof and was built with blocks of local 400-millimetre thick white stone with no cavity. The simply constructed (by Antonio) two-storey house had the kitchen and a cow shed on the ground floor, two bedrooms up a flight of stairs and an attic/food storage room in the ceiling.

Farm life in Friuli

My region, Friuli, was divided into Provincia Udine and Provincia Pordenone. In ancient times, the region was invaded by barbarian tribes from the Austrian side of the Alps—the Goths, Ostrogoths and the Lombardi—while the Turks used to land in Trieste and maraud across what is now Friuli and the Veneto. The inhabitants would escape to the swamps of what is now Venice, and over time, began building the foundations of the city that stands there now. The Romans came, and they called it Venezia Giulia and Aquilea after Julius Caesar. They reconstructed everything in the Roman model and

Left: Beppi's sister, Anna, performing the Polese children's regular duty, collecting water from the fountain in the piazza.

Below: Beppi's father, Antonio, after learning how to ride in Australia.

Below: Beppi's mother, Caterina, in the courtyard. The Poleses kept chickens and exchanged the eggs for essentials at the village store.

Below: Clockwise from top, Rosa, Anna, Rosa's husband, Ercole, Antonio and Caterina in the front yard.

introduced well-organised agriculture. They planted grapevines for wine, sorghum and wheat all across the region of Friuli.

As a child I would come out my gate on to the road and look across to a wall with grapevines behind it on a hill. Behind that were more hills, covered by a forest with chestnut and hazelnut trees, and in the distance a mountain range which rose to 2500 metres, where, much later I joined with the partisans.

Further up the hill I could see the house called 'La Dottora', where my father grew up. When I turned right, I would go past the neighbours' blocks of land. One family, the Rovere, had a very big house—five cows. We were good friends with them and helped them with their farming in exchange for potatoes and corn. They were my godfather and godmother and every Easter they would give me two-dozen coloured chicken eggs.

We had a block of land in front of our house, 2 kilometres away and another block at Fontaniva, about 4 kilometres away on the road to Sacile—this was really beautiful land, with a spring in the middle of it. In the second lot my father grew grass for the cow. To survive, you need potatoes, corn, *orzo*—which makes broth as well as coffee, and grass for the cows. In the winter you give them *fieno* (hay) made from the grass which we had dried during the summer.

My father grew white maize for polenta, which had much more flavour than the yellow stuff we use in Australia, and a smaller variety called 'cinquentino'. We used to fry the grains in lard to make popcorn. We also grew a little wheat, which gave us flour for pasta and a little for bread—we hardly ever had bread though. There were rows of cherry, apple and pear trees with vegetable plots between them—potatoes, pumpkins, tomatoes, spinach, sorghum and all sorts of herbs. We never needed to buy vegetables, which was a good thing because we couldn't afford to.

My father had a few grapes in the front of the house—merlot and about four other varieties. He made his own wine, mixing grapes from all of the vines, but because he used to ferment it with the stalks still on, it was pretty rough. The bitterness of the stalks I learnt to detect from the age of ten—I can still pick it in wines now. But it was only 8 per cent alcohol, so you could drink a lot of it. And he made a grappa too with *ruta* (a bitter medicinal herb know as 'rue' in English), which he grew in the garden—about 50 per cent alcohol. Whenever I had a sore stomach, my mother would give me a teaspoon. And I tell you what—I felt better straight away.

We had two cows, one pig and about twenty chickens, which were kept behind wire in the courtyard. These days you would call them free range. They gave us eggs, which were like money for us—my mother would exchange eggs at the local shop for things we couldn't grow ourselves, like salt and sugar. The chickens were very important, so we could only eat them when they stopped laying. That usually meant they were old, and so they were best boiled or stewed, *spezzatino di pollo*. We'd have chicken as a special treat with polenta sometimes on Sunday after Mass.

Later on, when I used to come home from doing seasonal work in hotels and would run out of money, my mother would use the eggs to buy cigarettes for me. She never did anything for herself—always working to provide food for us five children. She didn't smoke or drink wine, and she never even rode a bicycle. I tried to teach her once, but after that attempt she never tried again! Wherever she went, she walked.

My mother did tailoring of pants and shirts for local people, and they would pay her with food. She was also a kind of nurse. The doctor would call her any time somebody needed looking after, and she acted as a midwife, delivering babies under the supervision of the village doctor. When somebody died, the family would call her to dress the dead man or woman, to prepare them for the burial. The dead person would be displayed in the kitchen in an open coffin with a candle in each corner the only light. Once, she took me to see the dead body of another villager; I was very scared when this happened and had frightful dreams.

When all the children were living at home they worked as hard as Caterina and Antonio. 'With my three sisters, Teresina, Anna and Rosa, and my brother Gigi, we used to do odd jobs for people, picking potatoes, corn, and so on, and they would pay us with a share of what we picked.'

Our main job was collecting the water from the fountain in the middle of the village, which caused big arguments. There was no water in the house and we had to go to the fountain in the piazza, about 500 metres away. We used

CIMON DEL CAVALLO
2251

BARCIS

PIANCAVALLO

GIAIS

COSTA

MARSURE

PEDEMONTE

AVIANO

VILLOTA

CASTELLO
D'AVIANO

VENICE – 100 km

N
W   E
S

what they called a 'thampedon', a curved piece of wood that you put over your shoulders, with a hook on each side and a bucket over each hook. Being children, we couldn't carry much weight, so we had to go more often, back and forth. It was very hard and often they would make me do it because I was the smallest. We would also walk the cow to the fountain for water.

The youngest member of the family, christened Giuseppe but known since birth by the diminutive Beppi, made his own particular contributions to the family's nutrition.

At the foot of the mountain near our village is a spring called Gorgazzo, with water gushing out from under a huge rock. That creates a brook that runs through the town and joins up with another brook from a spring called Santissima about 2 kilometres away. Together they form a river called the Livenza, and that was where I would go fishing with my spear in the summer and autumn. I was looking for eels and marson, which are like small catfish, about 10 centimetres long, which hide under stones. They taste good fried in lard.

I carried a sharpened fork attached with wire to a long stick. I would wade in the water up to my thighs wearing shorts, always moving upriver so I had a clearer view, with a large tin container tied to my belt, spearing the marson as they moved between the stones. I also carried a small net attached to the back of my belt to catch small trout and slimy eels, whose heads you had to cut off as soon as you caught them to stop them wriggling away.

In the forest I'd collect chestnuts and wild herbs, especially gallinella, and mushrooms—porcini or smaller ones called 'chiodini', which I love. You had to be careful with wild mushrooms. A few people in the village died from eating the poisonous ones. My mother had a trick—she'd start cooking the mushrooms and then put her gold wedding ring in the mixture. If the ring went dark, the mushrooms were poisonous, so then she knew to throw them away. She'd cook the good mushrooms with garlic until all the moisture was out and they went crunchy.

After the rain, I would catch snails in the bush under the nettles. To eat them, you must first leave them in a bucket with polenta flour for two days to clean them out. Then boil them, pull them out of the shells, clean them and leave them to soak in water and vinegar. Then cook them as you would a *spezzatino* (stew)—with not too much tomato—and serve them with polenta.

In October, in the Autumn, thousands of small birds—*becacci* (woodcocks), *merli* (blackbirds) and *canarini* (canaries) would start migrating across our mountains to escape the cold of the north. The local hunters would put a kind of glue on the tree branches to trap the birds—when they stopped to rest, they got stuck. But I had a different way to catch the sparrows in the winter snow.

We would make a kind of cage, a square frame of wood and chicken wire, 1.5 x 1.5 metres; clear a patch in the snow about 2 x 2 metres, and put some wheat in the middle of the patch. Then we'd prop up the cage with a stick, at a 45-degree angle, over the wheat, and tie a long string to the bottom of the stick. The string needed to be pretty long, long enough to reach through the window into the kitchen, where we were hiding from the birds. When they came to eat the wheat, we would pull the string, the cage came down, and we had our birds, ready to pluck and put on the skewer with pieces of pancetta, sage and garlic. We'd pan-fry them until they were crisp and eat them with polenta.

I did six years schooling in San Giovanni, five years plus one repeat, and I left when I was eleven. The school was 1 kilometre from the house, and I would walk there with my cousin Giovanni—there were about twenty children altogether in the school. In winter, my mother would put butter on my lips against the cold. We learnt Italian at school, because we spoke dialect at home—ours was a cross between the Friuli and Veneto dialects.

I wasn't very marvellous as a student. My report in 1934 said 'sufficiente' in 'Storiae cultura fascista'—Fascist law and virtues. Mussolini was running the country in conjunction with King Vittorio Emmanuelle, and at school every Friday we had to put on a uniform—black cap, shirt and tie, green shorts and socks, and black shoes—group together and march to Fascist music. They called us *figli della lupa* (cubs of the she wolf).

There were those in our neighbourhood opposed to the Fascists—people who would say 'the bloody Fascisti' and so on. There were about half a dozen people in the village who had Fascist membership and if one of them heard you say anything bad about the *Fascisti*, they would report you to the Fascist officials who would take you to their office in Polcenigo and give you castor oil to drink. My father always kept his mouth shut about politics. People who were considered violent were sent away to political prison in the south. We called it 'confini'.

When I finished school, I went to work in a bicycle shop with my cousins Marco and Feruccio Quagia. Then my mother sent me to study at night school to get an architect design certificate. We had a neighbour who had studied at the same school. I had to walk to Polcenigo and there were no street lights—I used to be really scared. But I finally got the certificate.

But Beppi's real education for the first fourteen years of his life was in the ways of food: how to find it, grow it, nurture it, flavour it, share it and—when necessary—kill it. The highlight of the year for young Beppi was December, because that was when all the children joined in 'The Day of the Pig'—and had the chance to feast on meat.

Home smallgoods.
From pig to salami

Early in the year we got a piglet which we fed on whey from cheese making mixed with grass, leftover vegetables, boiled grasses and the husks of the wheat. That pig had a nice life. It ate better than the humans because it was going to become our supply of meat through the following winter. It would end up weighing about 150 kilograms—nothing like the 250 kilograms of the pigs they use for prosciutto, but pretty healthy.

In December, my father would announce that the pig was fat enough, and it was time to send for the *porthiter*—that's the pork butcher who goes from family to family during the winter. In fact, it was my father's cousin, Angelo,

who lived about 4 kilometres away. We would pay him in clothing made by my mother.

On the appointed day, we kids got up very early (about 3 am) to boil a lot of water in a big copper pot. The butcher would arrive with his knives, his mincers, his spices and his son, who was learning how to do the job by watching, the way Angelo had learnt from his father.

He would stick the pig through the heart with a long knife, and let the blood run out into a bucket. Then we would drag it out of the pen by the back legs and ears and lay it on top of a large box.

We would then pour hot water from the pot over the skin, to soften the bristles so they could be scraped away with a knife. (The hot water should not be too hot or it will burn the skin and ruin the lard, and when you are scraping you must be careful not to cut the skin.)

Then Angelo would hoist the pig up into the air with its head hanging down and its back legs apart. He would slice down through the belly, reach in with his hand and gently take out the intestines, leaving the liver and kidneys attached to the spine. You must be careful not to cut the guts or stomach or you will contaminate the meat.

He washed the guts with tepid water and vinegar. Then he turned them inside out like a flower, scraped the dirt from them and washed them properly with warm water and vinegar, so they could be used as skin casing for sausages. The pig didn't have enough intestines for all the sausages he was going to make, so he would also bring horse intestines preserved with salt to be a casing for the pork meat, which he would also wash well with warm water and vinegar.

Then he would start slicing up the pig and laying the pieces on a big table, ready for deboning, mincing and spicing. He would add salt and pepper and different flavourings, such as cloves, nutmeg, cinnamon, garlic and wine, according to what the family liked best. Then he would force the spiced mince through a funnel into the sausage casings.

There was a use for every single part of the pig and that became our meat supplies for the next eight months. The blood we would sauté with onion, sultanas and cinnamon to make a sausage filling. The belly became pancetta. The stomach, turned inside out, would be tripe. The liver would go into figadelle sausages and the lungs would become luganeghe sausages. We would eat them first.

The nose, ears, skin and sinews would be minced to become cotechino sausage (which we called *muset*). It is very tough, and you must boil it for about three hours, then slice it and grill the slices. We'd serve it with horseradish or just eat it. My mother would cook pasta and *fagioli* (beans) in the water it had been boiled in.

The neck would be a gift to neighbours, because they had given us a piece of pork when they killed their pig. You can roast the neck with rosemary and garlic, and add a splash of vinegar to reduce the fattiness.

The best meat is the lean meat which comes from the legs, and it is mixed with garlic, wine and cinnamon and goes into salami. The salami would hang in our kitchen for about two months, drying out from the warmth of the open fire, and then we would hang it in our cellar. We left that till last to eat. The fat would be used for most of our cooking. We never used olive oil because it was too expensive.

My mother used to keep the back leg bones of the pig and every time any of us had aches in our muscles, a twisted ankle or a dislocated shoulder, she would cut the bone and massage the marrow into the sore spot as a salve. I was often prone to those injuries because I was very energetic and always running around the countryside barefoot and the ground was all gravel. Evidently, the marrow of the pork has some chemical that penetrates—now they would use Dencorub. The other bones would go into a barrel, under salt, to be boiled to add flavour to soups. The skin was also beautiful boiled with vegetables.

That day was a feast day for us, because while we were making the salami, we'd be cooking and tasting the meat to adjust the flavour. We used to stuff ourselves as well as the sausages. It was fantastic.

For the children, there were many joyous moments like that. For the parents, it was a constant struggle to keep them clothed and fed. The time came when Beppi had to stop being a child and contribute to the financial wellbeing of the family.

When I was fourteen, my mother found a job for me in Milan, with a fellow from the village who was working in a factory where they made parts for

locomotives. The day came when she took me on the bus to Sacile to put me on a train.

At first I was excited at the idea of the trip. I had never been on a train before. We couldn't afford even bicycles at the time. But then, as the train was arriving, I realised I didn't want to leave her. I was much closer to my mother than my father. He was away most of the time and when he was around he didn't show much emotion, he was a severe man.

My excitement disappeared and panic started at the thought of being separated from my home. I hung onto my mother's skirt so tight and when the whistle came for the train to start off, I started to cry. She cried too. She put me on the train and closed the door. I sat huddled in a corner. I didn't move until the train arrived in Milan, scared of the rumbling noise of the carriage, and only got up to go to the toilet.

A skinny farm boy climbs off the train in Milan, overwhelmed by the crowds, jumping at every sound, and wondering where to go next. He looks around for the only friendly face he will see in that confusing crowd, a family friend from the nearby village of Fontaniva who had found him the job in the factory. A voice comes from the crowd on the platform, 'Beppi? Beppi?', and he finds the man who will take him to his new life in Via Vittor Pisani in Milan.

That life will soon be overtaken by the events taking place around him. It was 1940—the year that Hitler invaded Denmark, the Netherlands, Belgium and France. Most significantly for the young Beppi Polese, it was the year that Mussolini entered the war.

Left: Polcenigo, the communal centre where the Polese family lived, in the mountains of Friuli.

Left: Beppi's cousins, Beppino and Franco Sormani. Beppino is dressed in the uniform of the *Balilla* (the Fascist Party youth group).

Above: Beppi's mother, Caterina, and one of Beppi's three sisters, Anna, outside the family home.

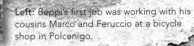

Left: Beppi's first job was working with his cousins Marco and Feruccio at a bicycle shop in Polcenigo.

Left: The rural community of Polcenigo in the foothills where Beppi grew up.

Below: The Polese children, clockwise from top left, Rosa, Beppi, Teresina and Anna. (Beppi's other sibling, Gigi, was away working in Verona at the time.)

Below: Beppi's father, Antonio, with a glass of the rough blend he made himself, at the kitchen door.

Home cooking

POLENTA

Polenta was the gut-filler of my childhood diet, doing the job that pasta or rice does in other parts of Italy. Most days we had it with breakfast, lunch and dinner. The trick was to make it more interesting by making flavoursome sauces to put over it. I remember that in winter, when I was young, every family in the village had polenta cooking in their houses in the evening and if I went outside, the air was sweet with the smell of the cooking polenta coming out of everyone's chimney.

My mother's basic recipe involved slowly adding 600 g of the ground white maize flour (what is commonly called 'polenta' really should refer to the finished dish, not the flour) to 2 litres of water, ½ litre of milk and a fistful of salt boiling in a big copper pot. You stir as you add, so it doesn't form lumps. Then turn the heat down to a simmer, and stir with a wooden spoon for at least 30 minutes and up to 45 minutes until the polenta is smooth and thick—not too thick though, it should be like porridge—and comes away from the side of the pot. Giving an exact recipe is tricky because we cooked it all by 'feel'. We never measured anything and didn't use a whisk to make this—it was stirred with a wooden spoon until it was the right consistency and this took practice. Near the end of cooking we would wet the wooden spoon so the polenta wouldn't stick to it. Remember that the polenta will get thicker and thicker as it cooks so you have to allow for this by not adding too much maize flour at the beginning. Also some people like their polenta maybe a little bit thicker (in which case you leave it on the heat for longer) or maybe a little bit thinner than others so it is up to you to cook it as you like.

Then we would pour the finished polenta, which looked like a large soft cake, on a wooden board (but you can use a tray with no sides), then cover it with a wet tea towel to keep it warm. That would go into the middle of the table.

People can cut slices as they like. Mother liked to use a string—she pulled it down through the polenta across and lengthways to form the sign of a cross and make four slices. If you use a knife to cut the polenta, make sure it is wet, or the polenta will stick to it (no need to wet the string, though).

Polenta can be eaten straight away or left to cool and used the next day.

If using the next day, you cut it in slices, and you can grill or pan-fry slices in lard, butter or olive oil until crisp. We would then eat it with something tasty like cheese or uncooked salami.

Now here are some improvements:

POLENTA CON IL MUSS

Mum would make what she called a 'muss' to pour over the polenta. It was a kind of béchamel sauce. She would cut some pancetta into small pieces and fry it in a pan with a little lard (you could use butter) until crisp—about 3 minutes—then add thickly sliced salami and cook it for 2 minutes more, or until it has softened (actually Mum would cook the meats together but because the salami in Australia tends to go hard when cooked for too long, it is better to add it near the end). Then she'd take out the salami and pancetta, throw in some sage leaves, and slowly add a little flour to the frying pan, stirring it into the fat until it was a smooth paste. She'd then add some milk, stirring all the time. She'd put the salami and pancetta back in at the last minute and mix it in with the white sauce. She would give each of us a plate with a slice of salami, a little pancetta and the sauce, then we would help ourselves to the soft polenta from the middle of the table. Our father would sometimes give us a glass of his wine, although mostly we drank water. My mother never drank wine.

Note: Slice salami thickly. Outside Italy it's hard to find soft salami that adds as much flavour to the *muss* as the Friulani salami that we used; salami from Friuli and the Veneto are very tasty raw, but cooked, when they lose a lot of their moisture (they are about 30 per cent fat), they are even tastier and are particularly good with polenta. Modern salami tends to have too much salt. You could use sopressa instead, but it doesn't need to cook as long.

POLENTA CONDITA

This means polenta with 'condiments' and can be prepared using soft, just-cooked polenta or the previous day's (which is firm) polenta.

If using soft polenta, put it into a large greased baking dish. If using firm polenta, slice it into even-sized chunks using string or a thin, sharp wet knife, and place the pieces in the greased baking dish. Heat them in a 180°C oven for 5 minutes or until very crisp, then remove. Put a layer of sliced montasio, fontina or asiago cheese over the polenta, then slices of tomato or gorgonzola cheese and a dob of butter. Put the baking dish back into the oven and cook for about 3 minutes until the cheese has melted, then serve immediately. We used to do this in a pan over an open fire. After sprinkling with cheese we'd cover the polenta with a lid and cook until the cheese melted.

Really, you can make the condiment(s) using whatever is in your pantry—garlic and onion with olives and herbs such as rosemary, oregano or marjoram, for example—or tuna and peas, some ricotta, bacon and sage or cooked leeks, spring onions or cabbage. Tinned tomatoes are always good and the topping could even be as simple as a bit of peperoncino and some anchovies. You always need some sort of cheese though and you can use ingredients that are leftovers.

PASTICCIO DI POLENTA

This dish is always made using firm, cold polenta. You cut the polenta into small pieces (about 3 cm even-sized chunks), then mix it in a greased baking dish with small pieces of cheese and cook until hot in a 180°C oven. You can also add some chopped salami or tuna or anchovies to the mixture—or any type of cooked fish, with bones removed, is good. If you like, you can also add a little garlic and parsley, or even better, chopped celery leaves to it. The most important thing here is, as with most recipes, to find out what your own preferences are and don't just slavishly follow the recipe.

To make the sauce, fry sliced onions, some chopped prosciutto or pancetta and garlic in butter until they begin to turn brown. Add a chopped tomato for each eater (or 2–3 tinned tomatoes, broken up with a wooden spoon) and a pinch of basil and oregano (not too much because it's powerful) and simmer the mixture for 30 to 40 minutes or until well-reduced. Add the tip of a teaspoon's-worth of sugar if you like. Pour the sauce over the polenta in the dish, slice some asiago, fontina, montasio or mozzarella cheese over the sauce, and then put the dish in the oven (at about 140°C) for 5 minutes, or until the cheese has melted. You can also add some tomato and basil on top of the cheese before you put it in the oven, if you like, to make the dish look better. Serve immediately.

ZUPPA. STOCK FOR SOUP

To make a basic stock, mum simmered the vegetables (chopped onions, carrots, a lot of celery, bay leaves, thyme and chopped tomatoes) first in about 10 litres of water to give it a bit of flavour, then she added broken up bones from chicken, beef or pork. The pork bones would have been preserved in salt—when a pig was killed every part was kept for later use including the bones. The stock would simmer for 3 or 4 hours, then she would strain out the solids and simmer the stock until it was reduced and flavoursome.

If she was making soup straight away, she'd take out the bones, but leave in the vegies, and add more vegetables (pumpkin, peas, leeks, garlic, spinach, potatoes, cabbage and corn sometimes) plus some big white beans (which had been soaked overnight if they were dried). She would often add *corita* (pork skin), which greatly improved the flavour.

The stock produced by this method looks murky, and you may prefer to make a clear stock (as restaurants do). This procedure is a bit more complicated. First, you boil the bones for 10 minutes, drain and throw away that water (which will be discoloured by blood). Then you smash up the bones and throw them into 8 litres of water with chopped onions, carrots, celery and bay leaves or any herb to your liking, plus—here's the important difference—5 or 6 eggshells and a drop of sweet white sherry. The eggshells have the chemical effect of clarifying the liquid.

Simmer for 4 hours, skimming off any scum that appears on the top. Let it cool, then carefully strain out all the solid ingredients. Store the stock in the refrigerator—it should be lightly jellied by the next morning. You can freeze this stock and use it to make *zuppa pavese* or risotto (see chapter 2) or consommé (see chapter 6).

Note: For *consomme restretto*, after straining the stock, you simmer it for 15–20 minutes, to reduce it. This accentuates the flavour. Remember that you should never salt sauces or stocks or consommé until the very end of cooking and then, only if it is really required.

FRICO

This is a typical dish, a potato bake, from Friuli.

Put a little pancetta and butter in the bottom of a baking dish, then a layer of sliced onion and a layer of sliced raw potatoes (some people include cooked prosciutto or bacon and some use slices of tomato as well). Pour in boiling chicken or beef stock, just enough to cover the potatoes. Bake in a 160°C oven for 10 minutes. Fry pieces of pancetta until they are crisp and spread them over the top of the potatoes. Then spread thick slices of tasty cheese (asiago or montasio) and bake for another 10 minutes. Some people also like to put a layer of thickly sliced tomatoes on the cheese. Vegetarians would leave off the pancetta.

FRITTOLE

These are soft pastries we would eat at Easter—though not, of course, during Lent because they were cooked in lard. Mix 1 kg of flour, 2 teacups of milk, 1 teacup of sugar, 1 teacup of sultanas, a pinch of grated cinnamon, ½ espresso cup of marsala (for flavour) and ½ espresso cup of rum or grappa (for kick). Add a pinch of yeast, and keep stirring and adjusting with additional milk or flour until it's a smooth batter that is runny but thicker than pouring cream, then set aside in a warm place for a couple of hours.

Heat some lard or pork fat in a frying pan (you could use olive oil) and then drop soup-spoonfuls of the mixture into the pan so it sizzles. Turn after 1 minute and fry for another minute. Scoop the golden pastries out and put them onto a clean tea towel or a paper towel.

They taste great cold, the next day.

PASTA ALL'UOVO E SPEZZATINO DI POLLO

Whenever a hen stopped laying eggs, we could have chicken for a Sunday feast, which came in two courses. Mum would go to early Mass, then make pasta when she got back home. She'd put 1 kg of flour in a mound on the wooden table, make a well in the middle and break in 8 eggs (the general rule for pasta is 1 egg per 100–120 g of flour). Then she'd add ½ eggshell of melted butter and two ½ eggshells of warm water and mix it all with her hands.

The trick to making fresh pasta is in the kneading and the rolling out with a rolling pin. You have to fold the dough back onto itself and roll it out again and again until your shoulders ache. Put the dough in a bowl, cover with a tea towel and let it rest in a warm place for an hour.

Finally, break the dough in a couple of pieces and roll each out as thinly as possible, sprinkle on more flour, then roll up as a tight cylinder—like a newspaper being delivered through your letter box, always sprinkling with flour to make sure it doesn't stick. Then cut across the roll with a sharp knife, making rings that can be opened out into noodles. How finely you slice will determine the width and therefore the name of the pasta (very thin would be tagliolini or trenette, medium would be fettuccine, thick would be pappardelle). Or you can skip the whole process and just buy fresh fettuccine.

Mum would separate them into noodles and lay them out on a tea towel, sprinkled with flour, and cover them with another tea towel. This way they didn't get so dry that they would break during cooking.

 Now the chicken. You've killed it, cut off the head, hung it to bleed for 15 minutes, plucked it, cleaned out the guts (keeping the liver and the giblets), burnt the skin to get rid of the last feathers (which adds a bit of barbecue flavour), then washed it. Or you've bought one already cleaned.

Cut off the drumsticks and the wings and chop the rest into 8–10 pieces, keeping the skin on, then toss all the bits in flour. Fry finely chopped onion, garlic, celery, rosemary and thyme in butter for 10 minutes, stirring occasionally, then throw in the pieces of chicken and brown the meat for another 5 minutes. (You can also do this with rabbit, or chopped up veal shoulder.)

Splash on 1 glass of white wine and simmer until it evaporates. Then add 8 large tomatoes (chopped small), 1 tablespoon of tomato paste, some basil and chilli, and continue cooking on a low heat (lid off) for half an hour or longer. You want to make a lot of sauce, a stew, so if it's reducing too much you can add more tomatoes or some chicken stock. Remove the pieces of chicken onto plates, putting a spoonful of sauce on each piece.

Now boil the pasta in salted water for 7 minutes, take it out, and put it into the sauce in the saucepan. Simmer the pasta for another 3 minutes so it absorbs some of the sauce, and serve with parmesan cheese.

Next, serve the chicken pieces with polenta, rice or mashed potatoes.

Note: Always simmer pasta in the pot with the sauce during the last stage of cooking so that it can absorb the sauce flavour. The general rule is 70 per cent of cooking time in boiling water, and 30 per cent cooked in the sauce.

CINGHIALE IN SALMI

There were *cinghiale* (wild pigs) in the hills near us, but my father was not one of the people who hunted them (he couldn't afford a gun). Occasionally, my family was given a shoulder of boar in exchange for clothing made by my mother. This rich recipe is also useful for deer, hare or pheasant—and in Australia it would work well with kangaroo.

If you don't like a gamey taste, you should first soak the meat in a mixture of 3 litres of water and ½ glass of vinegar for a few hours to moderate the flavour. This is not necessary if you are using a piece of pork, veal or beef from the butcher.

Marinate the meat for at least 24 hours in a large plastic or crockery bowl with chopped raw onion, garlic, celery, carrot, cloves, bay leaves, crushed juniper berries, cinnamon, pepper (even chopped chillies if you like) and enough red wine to cover the meat. The better the wine, the better the flavour—I used to like bardolino.

Take out the meat, dry it, cut it into pieces about 5 cm square and toss it in flour. Heat the marinade until it is simmering. In another pan, brown the meat in lard, butter or oil for 5 minutes, then add it to the simmering marinade with ½ litre of chicken stock. Simmer the mixture for at least 1½ hours until it has reduced into a thick rich sauce and the meat is tender.

You can serve it with polenta, mashed potatoes or rice.

ANGUILLA DELL'ALTO LIVENZA IN UMIDO

The name translates as 'eel from the high Livenza river in stew'. We used to catch them, but you can buy eels from good fish shops. The word 'umido' refers to a way of cooking that works equally well for pieces of chicken, beef or pork, so if the idea of eel makes you shudder, substitute the word chicken in your mind as you read this.

You need just over 1 kg of eels to serve four people. Wash and dry the eels and cut them into 8-cm long pieces, discarding the internal organs, head and tail. Wash and dry them with a clean tea towel. You can also slice the meat off the bones and use the fillets (though I find keeping the bone during cooking makes more flavour).

Put the pieces of eel in a bowl, cover with water and squeeze the juice of ½ lemon or a splash of vinegar over them (this reduces the sliminess), with a handful of rosemary, salt and pepper and put to the side.

Fry sliced onions in butter (or oil) until they are going brown, add 8 chopped ripe tomatoes and 1 tablespoon of tomato paste, a pinch of oregano, stir, and simmer the mixture for half an hour.

Take the eel from the bowl and pat dry, then flour the pieces (the flour helps to thicken the sauce) and fry them lightly in oil. Next, add them to the pan containing the tomato mixture. Splash with white wine and simmer for another 15 minutes to reduce the sauce a bit. Serve with polenta and a salad of boiled potato and onion, dressed simply with olive oil, vinegar, salt and pepper.

OSEI ALLO SPIEDO

This is quails with sage. First catch your bird (the name means 'little bird on the skewer'). We used sparrows and cleaned them ourselves, but you can buy ready-cleaned quails at the butcher. You can also use veal or chicken, in which case it is called 'scarpeti' which translates as 'the bird has flown away'. Lightly singe the skin of the birds over a flame, to give a barbecued flavour, then cut them in half.

Cut some pancetta into thick slices, about half the size of the bird pieces. On a wooden skewer, put 1 slice of pancetta, 2 sage leaves, then ½ quail, then repeat with pancetta, sage, ½ bird, sage and pancetta. To be precise, each skewer should end up with four ½ birds, 6 slices of pancetta and 12 sage leaves. You can also use very thin slices of pancetta to wrap each bird completely—this way they will keep moist and absorb flavour. You could cook these skewers on a barbecue for about 10 minutes, but I prefer to do them in the oven: lay the skewers in a baking dish, splash on some olive oil and spread a few rashers of pancetta over them, and bake at 180°C for 10 minutes.

Take the dish out of the oven, sprinkle ½ glass of white wine over the birds, and bake for another 5 minutes or so until the wine evaporates. Take the dish out of the oven, use a fork to pull the birds off the skewer onto a plate. Serve with polenta, over which you pour some of the juice from the baking dish.

INSALATA AL LEGUMI

For this you use mostly cooked vegetables that have cooled down. My mother liked a mixture of boiled potatoes, zucchini, beans, capsicums, chicory, carrot, raw radish and lambs' tongue lettuce. To cook the capsicums, roast them under the griller or in the flames of the stove until the skin goes black, let cool, strip the skin off, take out the seeds and slice. You can keep the slices overnight covered with a mixture of oil, a little vinegar and a pinch of oregano.

When you want to serve the salad, slice the cold, cooked vegetables and mix with freshly sliced raw celery. These days we would splash the mixture with olive oil, but my father loved a dressing called *soffritto*: you fry lard and pancetta until the pieces are crisp and sizzling, then pour a splash of white vinegar into the pan so the mixture goes whoosh. Stir and pour this over the salad. It tastes great but olive oil is better for the heart. We also used this same dressing with boiled borlotti beans, onions and some salt and pepper.

CHAPTER TWO

FROM VENICE TO VIENNA AND THE LABOUR CAMPS

THE TIMES
1941

THE WAR WAS NOT GOING WELL FOR THE ITALIANS. ITALIAN EAST AFRICA FELL TO THE SOUTH AFRICANS IN 1941. IN 1942, THE BRITISH DEFEATED THE GERMAN ITALIAN FORCES AT EL ALAMEIN. BY THE END OF SEPTEMBER 1943 SICILY HAD FALLEN.

Women were recruited to work in factories and rationing was in force. In 1942, Britain and America began bombarding Italian cities.

In 1941, Germany attacked the Balkans and Russia. Japan launched its attack on the United States at Pearl Harbour. Orson Welles first showed his classic study of the personality of power—and the power of personality—*Citizen Kane*.

Right: Beppi in the mountains above his village in the early 1940s.

An apprentice in wartime Milan

Teresina Polese was scared. She barely recognised the skinny, hollow-eyed kid walking towards her in the gardens near Milan zoo this Sunday afternoon as the happy and mischievous younger brother she'd seen a few months earlier in San Giovanni. She asked Beppi if he was sick. 'No', he said, 'but I'm hungry'.

Since being collected from the station by his family friend from Fontaniva, Beppi had been in Milan for six months, working fourteen hours a day, seven days a week in the factory job his mother had arranged for him through a contact in his village. Teresina, working six-and-a-half days a week as cleaner, cook and maid for a wealthy family, hadn't been able to meet up with him until now. And the change was alarming.

A few years earlier she'd been able to help her father when he turned up in Milan on the way home from Australia. She'd bought him a new suit. Now she realised she needed to save her brother from a fate much worse than embarrassment. He was so skinny, she knew if he kept on this way, he could become very sick. So Teresina came up with an idea that was to transform Beppi's life and set him on the path to his later triumph. He had never shown any particular aptitude for or interest in the hospitality industry, but if she could get him into a professional kitchen, at least he wouldn't starve.

This was 1941. Mussolini had brought Italy into the war on the side of Germany the year before, and he had introduced food rationing. I never had enough coupons ... some mortadella, one coupon; a jar of marmalade, one coupon; a loaf of bread, another coupon. That was my food for a week while I was cleaning up and greasing the machinery in this factory.

At night, the family I was staying with would give me a big bowl of *minestra di verdura* (vegetable soup). I slept on a foldout bed between their fridge and their stove. After they went to bed, I would sneak open the cupboard very quietly and pinch a piece of old bread, and eat it under the covers.

There was black market food around, but I couldn't afford it, even though I saved money by dodging my fare on the tram to and from the factory. I would hop off at each stop and get back on at the opposite end from the conductor.

Every couple of weeks I would bundle up my dirty clothes in a suitcase and send it by train to my mother. She'd wash them and send them back with a salami or some cheese hidden among them—but she'd keep this from my father, because back in San Giovanni they were as hungry as I was.

So when I finally saw Teresina one Sunday afternoon she became terribly worried, and she started thinking how she could help me. Her best friend Virginia had a boyfriend named Battista, a short guy with flat feet who worked as the head waiter in a hotel near the railway station—The Albergo Doria Svizzera. It wasn't a very grand hotel—about 50 rooms, more of a three star than a five star by today's classifications. But its owners had their own farm in Pavia with goats and pigs—and even though they didn't feed the staff that well, in such a kitchen, you can always find food—you test and pick while the chef is cooking.

So Teresina spoke to Battista, and he spoke to the owner, and it turned out they needed somebody to help in the kitchen. And so I started as an apprentice in the kitchen two days later. I did breakfast and lunch, and in the afternoon they dressed me in a coat and tie and I did room service. In the evening I was in the kitchen helping the chef.

I shared a room in the attic with one of the waiters. The owner was Signor Emoli—I don't think I ever heard his first name—he was a nice man with a big moustache. He showed me the basics of cooking. It was Milanese style, which was so different from what I ate at home that it was as if I was in another country. His favourite dish was *nervetti*, made from veal sinews. In that kitchen, during the war, I learnt to be very economical.

On Sundays, he would teach me about wine while we were transferring the bardolino wine from demijohns to bottles in the cellar, which we did by sucking it up a tube. There was no wine list, that was the only red he had,

CORSO HÔTEL SPLENDID

MILANO - CORSO VITTORIO EMANUELE, 15

Certificato N. 200

Il sottoscritto *Attilio Zaccheo*

del (1) *Albergo Corso*

in *Corso V.tt Em.le 15*

dichiara che il portatore del presente certificato

Signor *Poleti Giuseppe*

figlio *Antonio* e di *Traini Caterina*

di anni *16* nato a *Pozzenigo*

fu impiegato nel *mio Albergo* dal giorno

15 Novembre 1942 al giorno *9 Febbraio 1943*

in qualità di *secondo Cameriere*

Firma *Zaccheo*

Albergo Corso-Splendid
MILANO
ZACCHEO

Data *29 Febbraio 1943*

(1) Albergo - Ristorante - Bar - Offelleria ecc.

G.PONZINIBIO-MILANO

and I would bottle it with him every Sunday, unless he gave me special permission to meet Teresina in the park for a couple of hours.

His wife was not so nice. She made me scrub the wooden floors, sliding around with steel wool attached to one foot. Then she'd go round and find spots. 'Here, here, you didn't clean it properly, do it again.' Then I'd go over it again with wax.

I was on top of the world because I was surrounded by so much food. I felt that this was all I wanted to do for the rest of my life. After a couple of weeks, Battista asked my sister if there was something wrong with me. 'What, is he sick?' she asked. 'No, no', he said, 'but he never stops eating. I've got an ulcer, so sometimes I can't eat my portion, but then Beppi eats my portion as well as his own'.

They put me to work in the dining room and I began to learn how to be a waiter. When you do room service, you have to be prepared for anything. There was one old woman who would ring in the afternoon for her cup of tea and I had to take it up to her. I remember the smell of medication in the room, how I had to hold my nose against the smell.

At Christmas, Signor Emoli did something that impressed me so much I adopted the idea many years later when I opened my own place. He had all the staff sit down and with his son he cooked and served dinner for them— risotto, nervetti, roast pork, chicken. I felt very uncomfortable and I was too nervous to eat much, because I felt the owner has a position of respect and he should never lower himself to serve the staff. But he was different from every other hotel owner I met later.

One day, early in 1942, I was cleaning the floor in the dining room and I heard a loud roaring from above. I ran up to the attic, threw open the window and I could see these planes coming in very low and dropping bombs.

The RAF bombed Milan extensively—and in daylight—in October 1942 using 90 Lancasters flying at low level. It's highly likely there were some with Australian crews. Although aiming for the railway station, they were hitting all the houses around and fires were breaking out in the street.

Left: Beppi's second job in hospitality was at the Hotel Splendid, which he took hoping that its close proximity to Milan Cathedral would protect it from Allied bombing raids. It did.

These bombing raids kept happening and I realised the Doria was not a safe place to be. So I applied for a job at the Albergo del Corso Splendido (Hotel Splendid) near the cathedral, the Duomo di Milano, which seemed unlikely to be a target for the bombers.

Although the October 1942 bombing of Milan was extensive, the Allies appear to have gone out of their way to avoid the Duomo, the third largest Gothic cathedral in the world and the largest in Italy, a remarkable building on which work began in 1386 and was completed in 1809. It survived the war intact.

The Albergo del Corso was a place with about one hundred rooms that probably would be called a four star these days. I was a commis waiter, the next rank up from apprentice in the dining room. I shared a room in the attic with an Abyssinian (Ethiopian) by the name of Matteo. His body had a terrible smell and he used a very strong aftershave that produced a cocktail of odours. I was lucky that my bed was close to the window and I slept with the window wide open, even in winter.

The hotel owner was Commendatore Zaccheo, whose brother was associated with the high-ranking Fascists. No rationing for them, they had the best of everything. Mussolini stayed in the hotel a few times while I was working there, having dinner with about ten people in a private room, cooked and served by his private staff. I remember Mussolini as full of life, full of beans, moving all the time restlessly. They ate lasagne, cannelloni, roast meats and they drank the best wine—bardolino, chianti, valpolicello and white soave bolla.

It was more formal than the job at the Doria, and it seemed secure. They sent me to do an afternoon course in basic waiting and cooking, taught by a head waiter from the famous Excelsior Hotel in Venice. He showed me how to carve roasts; dissect quail, chicken and pheasant; how to slice fruit; and where to place the dishes and the glasses.

At first, my only problem at the Corso was a chef who had a very bad temper. Once, when the waiter who was my boss sent me to the kitchen to ask why an order was taking so long, the chef chased me up the stairs with a knife. Just as well I'd learnt to run fast, getting away from my father!

That was when I learnt that chefs work under tremendous pressure, and sometimes they don't behave like normal people.

After a few weeks Teresina asked me to see if there might be a job for her at the hotel. She was now working in a factory on the outskirts of Milan that made electrical wiring, and she thought that it was likely to be a bombing target (although, as it turned out, the bombers never went near it because the owners were English). I asked the head waiter and he said, 'Yes, we need someone to serve meals for the senior staff'—the head porter, the concierge and so on. Teresina came to work and she was well treated and happy. She stayed there until the end of the war, and then she went to work at a hotel in Switzerland where she met an Italian musician, a cello player from Florence, and later they married.

I would have stayed there too, but in February 1943 something happened that made me get out fast. By sheer luck I had been stationed in the most fashionable part of the dining room, where the head waiter always put the top customers, so we got more tips than any other waiters. Another commis, a nasty fellow, was very jealous and had a bad habit of being rude, insulting me during the service in the dining room. I tried to ignore him or laugh at him, but that made it worse.

One night after I had served drinks to a table, he pushed against my shoulder and swore against my mother, saying she was a prostitute and a cow. There is no justification for that sort of language. It was the worst thing that anyone could have said, to insult my mother. I lost my temper and I lifted my silver tray and crashed it on top of his head—in sight of all the customers. He fell down, and I thought I'd killed him. They sacked me on the spot.

I went straight home to San Giovanni and wrote a letter of apology to Commendatore Zaccheo, but it didn't help. So after four weeks I decided to see if I could get a job in Venice.

By the beginning of 1943 the war was turning. In February, the Germans surrendered in Stalingrad. In July, the Allies invaded Sicily, and in the same month, Mussolini was stripped of his power and imprisoned. In September, Italy surrendered to the Allies, and Germany seized Rome. In October, Italy declared war on Germany. Before long, these events would touch young Beppi Polese. At the end of 1942, at the age of seventeen, he left San Giovanni for Venice.

COMPAGNIA ITALIANA DEI GRANDI ALBERGHI
SOCIETÀ ANONIMA - SEDE IN VENEZIA

N.º 127

GRAND HOTEL
VENEZIA

ATTESTATO DI SERVIZIO

Cognome e Nome   POLESE GIUSEPPE

Paternità   di Antonio

Nato il   27 agosto 1925   a   S. Giovanni di Polcenigo

Domicilio   Polcenigo (Udine)

Giorno d'entrata   1 novembre 1943

Giorno d'uscita   16 gennaio 1944

Qualità dell'impiego   cameriere di portata.=

⟨ Raccomandabile ⟩

IL DIRETTORE DELL'ALBERGO

li   18 gennaio 1944

GRAND HOTEL - Venezia
Direttore

Spese

TIP. G. MAGNINI - TEL. 20-887

Beppi's reference from the prestigious Grand Hotel in Venice, where he learnt some unorthodox techniques, such as hiding roast chicken in the linen cupboard when there wasn't enough to eat.

An apprenticeship
at the grand hotels

Although I had lived 100 kilometres from Venice for most of my life, I had never been there. I was lucky to find work quickly, and to be moving up in the world, because I managed to get a job with the Gritti Palace, one of the greatest hotels in Italy, if not the world.

The Gritti Palace was exactly that—a palace built in 1525 for Andrea Gritti, the doge of Venice. Since becoming a hotel, it has built a reputation among the rich and famous as one of the most luxurious small hotels in the world. From Somerset Maugham to Woody Allen and Soon Yi, they've all stayed at the Gritti Palace, where young Beppi was to have his own brush with fame.

I realised the significance of the Gritti quite quickly. I was on room service duty one afternoon when I got a call from the bar to take a bottle of soave bolla and some glasses up to a room on the second floor. I knocked, opened the door and found the room was full of smoke, with the window closed. This bearded guy pointed for me to put the tray down on the table. I asked him if he wanted me to open the shutters to let out the smoke, he said no, asked me to fill the glass with wine, and kept on typing. They told me his name was Hemingway, some kind of writer from America.

Of course, I was still near the bottom of the waiter ladder working as a commis, and mostly serving in the Grand Hotel, another building connected by a bridge to the Gritti. At this point in the war, early 1943, the Grand Hotel was used by the Italian Government as an embassy, where high ranking officials of the Axis powers—Italy, Germany and Japan—held meetings and functions.

This was the place where I began to learn the little tricks to working as a waiter. The management didn't feed us very well, but I found it was possible to put aside a certain amount of food and drink that was not consumed by the customers.

There was an old well in the courtyard between the two hotels. If you were carrying some bottles of wine or brandy on a tray, you could tie a string round the neck of one of the bottles, dangle it down into the water, then tie the string to the metal framework over the well. When everyone had gone to bed, you would come back and pull the bottle up, cut the string and take the bottle to the attic to share with the other waiters.

When you were serving big parties, nobody kept a very close account of the number of chickens that were eaten. There was a long corridor from the kitchen to the dining room, with plenty of opportunities to pop one of the chickens from your tray onto the top of a linen cupboard, or cover a chicken with cloth, stick a knife through it and then pin it under a table so it was hidden by the long tablecloth. Then when everybody was gone, you'd go under the table or up to the cupboard and retrieve your bird. We wouldn't call it stealing. We never took anything from the customers, only from the kitchen. And we were hungry.

I also continued my education in understanding chefs. In the kitchen, the chef is king and the twenty people working for him were his slaves: one on soup, one on pasta and all entrées, one on fish, one on chicken, one on roast, one on vegetables, one on pastries and so on. And as far as he was concerned, the waiters were even lower. The Gritti chef would stand near the counter, examining every dish as it came past before he would let the waiter take it to the dining room. If one of us put a hand on his counter before he was ready, he would whack the hand with a cane.

That was all part of the fun of my life. And believe me, there wasn't much of that. We worked seven days a week—our only pleasure was that after dinner we would go to one of the nearby *osterias* that were run by people from our villages, and have some salami, a few drinks and play cards. For us waiters, the war seemed very distant, but everything changed in July of 1943.

THE TIMES
1943

ON 10 JULY 1943 TROOPS FROM PATTON'S SEVENTH AND MONTGOMERY'S EIGHTH ARMIES LANDED IN SICILY. THE DEFENDERS, THE ITALIAN ARMY AND THE SICILIANS, WERE LOATHE TO TURN THEIR HOMELAND INTO A BATTLEFIELD AND PUT UP LITTLE RESISTANCE. THIS BEGAN THE ALLIED ADVANCE THROUGH ITALY. ON 25 JULY MUSSOLINI TOLD THE FASCIST GRAND COUNCIL THAT THE GERMANS WERE CONSIDERING RETREATING FROM THE SOUTHERN PART OF ITALY. KING VICTOR EMMANUEL III ORDERED HIS ARREST AND IMPRISONMENT IN THE GRAN SASSO HOTEL IN THE MOUNTAINS IN ABRUZZO AND CHARGED MARSHALL BADOGLIO WITH FORMING A NEW GOVERNMENT. THIS NEW GOVERNMENT BEGAN SECRET NEGOTIATIONS WITH THE ALLIES IN SPITE OF THE CONTINUED PRESENCE OF GERMAN TROOPS IN ITALY.

A surrender to the Allies was signed by a representative of the Badoglio Government on 3 September and was announced to the world by Eisenhower five days later.

On 23 September, after a dramatic German parachute commando raid on the prison in which he was being held, Mussolini declared the Republic of Salo (which he named after the Italian town on the Lago di Garda) would continue the fight on the Axis side. This new northern government called up all young men to fight against the Allies.

Betrayal. Vienna and the labour camps

I didn't want to fight for the Fascists. We didn't like them at all. And by this time my brother Gigi, who had been in the parachute corps, was fighting with the Allies and the Eighth Army as they advanced northwards through Italy. If I joined Mussolini's army I would be fighting against my brother.

At this time, the head waiter of the Grand and the Gritti, Carlo Cipollato, a Venetian, came up with an idea of how we might avoid having to fight for the Republic of Salo. He had a good association with the head of the German Embassy, named Von Plessen, who was willing to write letters of recommendation for us to go to Vienna and work at a hotel near the Opera, I can't remember its name. We were waiters, not soldiers, and this way we could continue our work, out of the reach of Mussolini. I told my mother and father, and they accepted it.

So with Cipollato and my friend Alberto Giacomello, another young commis from Friuli who was working with me at the hotel, I caught the train from Verona, headed for Austria. We were very happy, joking around, until we reached the Brenner Pass. We had to get off the train at the checkpoint and show our papers to the German border guards. For some reason they took Cipollato to another room. There were SS officers in black uniforms buzzing around, and one looked at our papers and then, to our horror, tore up the letter from Von Plessen.

Then they took Giacomello and me back to the train line and made us climb onto a cattle wagon that was full of prisoners—Jewish, Croatian, Russians, women, children. It was very cold, and we had no way of eating, drinking or even going to the toilet. Twelve hours later we arrived in Vienna—but hardly in the way we'd intended. It was night-time and they loaded us onto a truck and took us to a labour camp near the Prater amusement park close to the River Danube. The labour camp contained rows of large wooden huts, surrounded by barbed wire, with watchtowers at either corner and a large guarded gate for entry and exit.

I don't know what happened to Cipollato, or why we were separated—all three of our names were on the letter, but he disappeared. We didn't think about it too much at the time, we were just confused and frightened. We had no idea what was going to happen to us. Later, I heard that at this stage of the war, the Germans were capturing foreign civilians to work in factories so their own men could fight.

They separated the Jews and took them to another part of the camp, then pushed us into a big shed, where there were men sitting around playing cards by candlelight. They pointed to some bunks where we could put our bags (full of our best jackets, shirts and pants so we could make a good impression as waiters). They gave us a bit of soup and told us to go to sleep. As soon as the guards went, each one of the men playing cards pulled out a knife and put them on the table. Not suprisingly, we were confused and very scared.

Next morning they gave us a piece of brown bread and something that was supposed to be coffee, made with roasted seeds. Then Giacomello and I, with four guards, went by tram to a factory called Optische Werke in the twenty-first circle (Vienna is organised in a spiral shape, the first circle being the centre of town, the twenty-first on the outer edge.) The factory made optical equipment, like binoculars, microscopes and gun sights. The guards came back in the evening to escort us back to the camp.

We worked in that factory for about three months. After a couple of weeks they decided they could trust us to take the tram there in the morning without the guards, and they relaxed the supervision in the camp. Even so, I never thought of escaping.

The Americans were bombing Vienna in the early mornings—they'd let us out of the camp, but we had nowhere to hide. I remember I used to cover my head until the planes disappeared—an instinctive reaction I guess. They never bombed the camp—or the amusement park.

I got to know a Yugoslav prisoner who had a special understanding with the guards whereby he was allowed out on Sundays to go and work in a beer garden in the Prater—we were civilian not army prisoners. He hired my best sports coat from me—paid me in food and cigarettes—and then he asked Giacomello and me if we'd like to come and work with him. We applied to the camp commandant and he gave us six-hour permits.

We found ourselves carrying jugs of beer in this place with about twenty-five tables, and I was fascinated that they had telephones on each table. A man could find out the number of a girl at another table and then phone and ask if she'd like to come over and join him. Although we served the beer, we never collected money for it—it was a pick-up joint. There was an oom-pah band and a jolly atmosphere, surreal considering that by this time Germany was losing the war and the city was growing more and more chaotic.

One morning in February 1944 the foreman came to us and said he had an order to double the production from the factory, and if we could work faster we would get a bonus. We worked harder and at the end of the month we were waiting for this bonus and wondering what they were going to give us—since we weren't paid money anyway. We thought the bonus might mean that the food would improve, but it stayed the same—a lot of potato soup, a lot of flour balls, a lot of cabbage. When we asked him, he said, 'Oh no, you haven't achieved the quantity of production we need'. We worked harder again and still nothing happened. So we slowed down. Then he threatened us: 'You're comfortable here, we're pretty easy on you, but unless you produce more, we'll have to send you away to the Hungarian border to dig tank trenches'.

We thought he was bluffing, but a few days later he came to us and said, 'Stop work, pick up your stuff and get on the truck. You're going to Hungary'.

Giacomello stayed behind—maybe he didn't seem as rebellious as me. I used to talk back to them, and I'd complain and send the food back. I remember this sweet they used to give us, flour and sugar beet as big as a tennis ball. I complained about the food.

They drove about twenty to thirty of us in wagons 250 kilometres to the south towards the Hungarian border with armed guards accompanying us. At six in the morning they would wake us up, give us a bit of coffee and bread with lard spread on it, and hand us picks and shovels. They set us to digging long trenches, a couple of metres deep, which were designed to stop Russian tanks from crossing into Austria. The guards watched us from the edge of the trenches. Because there was a shortage of food they would shoot anyone who couldn't continue working.

At midday we would stop work and queue up with aluminium plates to get our ration of soup. If there was any left in the bottom of the pot at the end, we would fight over the dregs. It was a terrible scene, men using their hands, slurping up bits of potato, cabbage, beans. You have no dignity left when you're that hungry.

I made friends with this Venetian fellow called Federico Centasso and at night we started talking about ways of escaping from there.

Escape to the partisans

We kept looking at what the guards were doing and we realised that while there were a lot of them standing around the trenches as we were digging during the day, there were not many of them outside the compound after dark.

We waited for a night when there was no moon, then we sneaked out and went into the forest very slowly. After we had gone about 300 metres we stopped and hid in the bushes because it was starting to get light.

No guards seemed to be coming after us, so we waited and tried to get some sleep until it got dark again. Then we started walking, staying away from roads. This continued for four days—sleeping on the ground under bushes during the day, walking at night, hiding every time we heard a car or truck, drinking water from streams in the forest.

Our only food was raw sugar beet that had been left behind in the fields by crop workers. I don't recommend them—they are pinkish outside, white inside, tough and slightly sweet. But they were all we had.

We didn't have much of a plan—just to try to get back to Vienna, and eventually we saw some road signs that told us we were going in the right direction.

When we reached a forested area on the outskirts of the city, we heard the sounds of planes overhead. We decided we'd better run because it looked like the planes were coming towards us. So we ran away as fast as we could and hid on the side of a ridge. The planes began dropping bombs and one hit the hut we had been heading for and it exploded. We looked at each other and said, 'Jesus, we were so lucky'.

Then Centasso did something stupid. He told me the area we were walking through was close to a concentration camp for women. 'My girlfriend is in there', he said. 'So what!', I answered. He said, 'I'd like to go and see her'. 'What do you mean', I said. 'We just escaped from a prison camp, and you want to go back in? You're crazy!'

But he insisted. He thought that in the general chaos at the time, he might be able to sneak in through the barbed wire and sneak out again without being seen.

So we made an arrangement. I would go to an area close to the factory we had worked in, and keep dropping into a café that we both knew about. If he was able to see her and get away, he would come and try to find me there.

I did see him again—about four weeks later. He turned up at the café one night; he was very skinny and his hair had fallen out. He told me he had been captured trying to get into the women's camp, and assigned to do road works in the snow outside Vienna. He had practically no food, and he said the prisoners who collapsed at their work were just shot by the roadside. He managed to escape and came looking for me. He looked terrible, and I shared my food with him and introduced him to my new friends.

At the café I had made friends with some other men who were also on the run. They were mostly Greeks who were using the café as a base for selling black market stuff. They were fugitives like me, and they were very good to me. Those kind of people don't look at you as if you are an Italian or a Jew. They just knew you were someone who needed help. They fed me and showed me how I could sleep under bridges, or break the lock on a shed in a builder's yard and find shelter. And they told me how I could go around during the day without being bothered by the police or the military. If I looked healthy they'd ask me why I wasn't working, so I had to look injured. I bandaged my head and my arm and tied a length of board behind one leg so I couldn't walk properly. People ignored me because they thought I was a cripple.

The gang from the café asked if I would like to sell cigarettes for them. I said, 'Yes, what do I have to do?' 'You just go to the park', they said, 'stand there, and people come up and buy cigarettes from you'.

That seemed simple enough, but on my first day, one of my first customers was a soldier. He took a pack of cigarettes and then said he wasn't going to pay. I had a signal and started to whistle—within seconds eight of my friends came from different parts of the park—surrounded the soldier. He paid up very fast.

In all of this time, Giacomello had still been working in the optical factory, and the control over the civilian prisoners had become pretty relaxed. One afternoon he came into the café and he found me there. It was a great reunion.

And he told me the answer to a mystery. Our old travelling companion Cipollato, who disappeared when we were taken off the train at the Austrian border, was working as a waiter in a restaurant in Vienna.

So we went to see him. He was having a fine time and we began to get an idea of why he had been treated so much better than us when he introduced us to his nephew. The nephew was a high-ranking member of the SS—black uniform and everything. He was the son of Carlo's brother who was a high-ranking Fascist in Venice.

'Oh no!' we said. This was pretty scary, especially when the nephew recognised our names. 'Ah', he said, 'you are Giuseppe Polese, you are Alberto Giacomello. You guys are on a list we found when we arrested an Italian captain the other day and the Gestapo are looking for the people on that list'.

We told him the captain had spoken to us about the idea of returning to Italy. The captain said he was going to lead a group of Italians over the Alps, but he never came back to see us again after we had given him our names. We thought he was on the Italian side, but according to Cipollato's nephew, this captain was recruiting people to join the partisans and fight the Germans. 'Well, we didn't know that', we said.

We took Cipollato aside and said, 'You better tell your nephew not to do anything stupid'. He said he'd fix it for us, but we couldn't be sure. It seemed like the right time to think about ways of getting out of Vienna.

Giacomello had his own plan. He knew Austria was starting to repatriate civilian prisoners who were too sick to work. He'd seen it happen with some of the people in the camp. So he decided to injure himself. He made this horrible wound in his arm, and he kept rubbing it with sandpaper. He would go to the infirmary and they would bandage it, and then he'd pull

Above: Beppi's cousin, Giovanni (Nanni) Moleta, a partisan based high in the mountains around Piancavallo, above Polcenigo.

Above: Polcenigo

Above: Beppi dodged conscription into Mussolini's army by escaping to Austria, and thus avoided having to fight against his brother, Gigi (above), who was fighting with the Allies in the parachute corps.

off the bandage, scratch it raw again and rub salt into the wound. After a week or so it smelt horrible, but it worked. The commandant was happy to get rid of him and gave him the documents that would let him take the train home.

So I went with him to the station to say goodbye, both of us all done up in our bandages. His flesh was rotting. I was faking. Giacomello went through the gate, followed by a large group of people. I made a spur of the moment decision—I'll just put myself in the middle of them and see what happens.

I found myself on the other side of the gate and in the confusion, nobody asked for my papers. I got through and onto the platform. I hadn't been planning to escape just yet, but here was the opportunity. So I climbed underneath the train.

The black market people in the café had told me that under the carriages there are containers to hold air conditioning, and not all of them have compressor machinery inside. This turned out to be right. I squeezed into an empty container. The train pulled out, and I was looking down at a snow-covered track a few centimetres from my face, with the noise of the wheels in my ears.

It was very cold, and the wind kept blowing snow into my face. I was so elated to be getting away that it took me a couple of hours to realise that if I didn't find some way to get inside the train, I would freeze to death.

When it stopped at a small station with no guards, I climbed out and got into the carriage. There was a group of about thirty Italians there. I said, 'Can you please help me?'

It turned out they were the same large group of people who had sheltered me in the crowds at the station. They had escaped from Greece and had been travelling overland through Turkey, Albania and Slovakia to Vienna and were on their way to Italy. They'd lost most of their documents, but their names were on a list that had been officially approved in Vienna. 'What if I join your group?', I said. 'Otherwise I'm going to die under there.'

They were afraid of getting into trouble and it took a lot of pleading, but finally the leader of the group agreed to add my name to the list of people authorised to go back to Italy. And just as well he did, because on the way from Villach on the Austrian side to Tarvisio on the Italian side, the Germans searched under the train with reflectors and shot anyone hiding under there.

I got off the train with my companions at Tarvisio. The Italian authorities gave us food coupons and cigarettes, and we left the railway station. Then I hitched a ride on a truck to Sacile and walked the 10 kilometres to San Giovanni.

You can imagine my mother's joy when she saw me. My father was working in the fields, so only my mother was at home. All she knew was that the Germans had been looking for me since I escaped on the Hungarian border and she hadn't heard from me in the eight months since I left Italy.

I slept in the house that night, but I knew it would be too dangerous for my family if I stayed in the area. So a friend and I decided to go up the mountain and cut timber—partly so I wouldn't be at home and partly to make a bit of money. I borrowed a big sled and ropes from my father and, with my friend Crispino, we would go up for a few days at a time, get the timber and come sliding down again and hide the timber in the bushes. My father would come along to meet us with a cart pulled by our cow, load up the timber, and then we would go back up the hill again to cut some more.

The first time we went up, we were cutting timber when a band of *partigiani* (partisans) came out of the forest and asked us what we were doing. My cousin Giovanni Favret was in that group.

The third time we came down, we had just unloaded our timber when we were spotted by a German platoon. They didn't know who I was—which is a good thing because I was not legal, I had no permit—but they were picking up young men because a lot of the local fellows had gone up the mountain to join the partisans, who kept ambushing the soldiers.

The Germans made us join them in raids on the houses of people suspected of helping the partisans. We had to bring out all their stuff—food (wheat, corn, salami, prosciutti), clothes, furniture, even their cows. Then the Germans would burn the houses and keep the goods.

After we'd done this one morning, they took us into the village of Dardargo, and told us to stand against a wall. Two or three of them had machine guns pointing at us and I thought, 'God, they're going to shoot us right here'.

A group of local women came by, with buckets over their shoulders, heading for the fountain in the piazza—so I picked up a bucket from one of the women and walked with her around the corner, to a spot where the Germans couldn't see me. Then I got out of there—racing across gardens, over walls and over hills, and managed to get back home.

Then I heard from Crispino that the Germans were looking for people to work at the railway station. The Americans would bomb the station, and they needed to repair it constantly. If you worked there they gave you a permit—naturally enough because you had to walk through the German checkpoint. I got the job and the permit and I became legal. I would walk down to Sacile, and walk back at night. Then my father found me a place not far from Sacile staying with a friend of his he used to work with in the mines—he let me stay in his barn at night, sleeping on hay.

Then the Germans began a curfew at 5 o'clock—and I didn't have time to get to where I was sleeping from the railway station after work. I got very worried because I heard they were shooting people who broke the curfew. At that time life was very cheap. So I went back to San Giovanni and I hid under the bed upstairs for a couple of days, but I realised I had only one option now: I had to join the partisans.

I knew of a guy called Gianno who had contact with the partisans, and I went to his house. Two guys came to meet me around 2 am, and the four of us set off up the mountain on foot, carrying in our rucksacks some bread, salami, eggs and cigarettes. We were going to walk all night.

About 8 am we reached the village of Mezzomonte and they said to me, 'You wait here, we've got to do something'. Half an hour later they came back, pushing in front of them a man with his hands tied behind his back. I asked, 'What did he do?' They answered, 'We had orders from the captain to pick him up. We'll tell you later what he did'. And the five of us walked to the top of the mountain, where the partisans were camping in *casere*—huts used by people who bring their cows up the mountain in the summertime where they also made cheese. They told me this fellow was a spy, a collaborator. He was telling the Germans which families had sons up the mountain.

My mother told me that before I came back the Germans had picked up one family in San Giovanni and told them they better spread the word that

The mountains looming over Polcenigo where Beppi and the partisans took refuge between their raids on the Germans.

unless their sons came down and gave themselves up, they would shoot the father and mother. The three boys came down, and the Germans released the parents. But then they took the three boys down towards the river and made them dig a trench. They shot the three of them in the back of the neck and buried them together in the hole they had made. There's a monument there now, near the cemetery, to those three boys.

You can imagine the hatred up the mountain for collaborators. So they had a tribunal—the captain and six partisans questioned this guy. He confessed, and the day after they took him out and shot him.

By the time I joined the partisans, we never used our real names. We all had *nomes de battaglia* (codenames). Mine was 'Tagliamento', after a nearby river. They gave me a uniform and at first I had the job of standing guard through the night. The wind was whistling, I was very scared, and I didn't know what I was listening for. It wasn't hard to pick when it happened. All of a sudden I heard explosions all round the mountains. The Germans had set off mines that the partisans had left there. I ran down and gave the alarm, and all the partisans went up to the peak with their weapons and started shooting. The Germans didn't come any further.

We were in radio contact with the English and they used to send planes to drop chocolates, cigarettes, weapons, uniforms (the uniform I was given was English), dynamite and coupons, which were kind of IOUs that we were supposed to use with shopkeepers—'please supply the holder of this coupon with food and after the war you will be reimbursed by the Allies'. I don't know if anybody was ever reimbursed. We used to call a plane like this *la cicogna* (the stork)—because it was like the old story that the stork delivered babies.

Every two weeks, we'd come down from the mountain carrying dynamite and detonators, hide until the next night and then walk to the Sacile road. One night we couldn't find shelter and had to sleep outside in the snow. The dynamite was to booby-trap the roads, and that became my assignment. Two of us had to go down the mountain carrying these greenish plastic tubes full of explosives until we reached a road used by German trucks. Late at night, we would put dynamite and detonators into the trees on either side of the road—up to twenty trees at a time—with a wire going across the road attached to them. A German convoy would come along and the first car, which usually contained the officer in charge of the convoy, would trip the wire and set off the dynamite. And anything caught between the explosions—sometimes as many as thirty trucks—would go up in smoke.

But one night we had placed the mines and gone off to a safe distance, about 200 metres away, to check how it went. A heavy truck and an armoured car came along, hit the wires, but the dynamite didn't detonate. The Germans realised what was going on. They stopped the convoy and started shooting into the bushes all along the side of the road.

I never ran so fast in all my life. We ran for a couple of kilometres (over the fields, jumping over the ditches) and arrived at my uncle's place at Fontaniva early in the morning. He was working in the fields and I told him what had happened. He said, 'Get down in this ditch and I'll put some grass over you, and just stay there until it gets dark, because there are German platoons all around here'. And we managed to avoid them until night and then went back up the mountain to the camp.

By now the Germans had a pretty good idea where we were up in the mountains, and they kept trying to come up the hill to reach our camp, getting closer and closer. The captain said we'd better disband the group. 'Every one of you go back to your own place as quietly as you can, change into civilian clothes and stay in hiding until we call you back up here.'

When we came down we found the Germans in disarray, as the Allies were getting closer. It wasn't hard to keep out of their way. I hid my weapons, grenades and uniform in the forest.

When I was called back up the mountains again a few weeks later, I walked through Polcenigo with my Sten gun and grenade under my raincoat—which was really stupid. Once we were up there, we got the news that the Germans were in their trucks running away. It was in May, and the war officially ended on the eighth.

So we came down and occupied the local towns. We went around searching to see if there were any Fascists hiding in the area. Then we handed in our weapons and I went back to Polcenigo to find my parents.

It was supposed to be a happy time but there were many people who wanted revenge. The partisans picked up girls who had gone with the Germans and shaved their heads. Some of those who had helped the

Germans or informed on the partisans were taken out and shot. It was sad—sometimes it was simply a family feud—they hated another family and they reported them.

With my group I went to Vigonova and we picked up a fellow who really had been collaborating with the Germans, he was a spy—this had been proven. I went into the cellar where they had locked him up and I said, 'Why did you do that, were you crazy?' They took him behind the church and shot him.

I didn't want revenge. I just wanted to get back to work. I asked my mother for some money for food, climbed on my bicycle and headed for Venice.

Following page: Beppi (right)—codenamed *Tagliamento*—with two fellow partisans during the war. Most of their supplies were air-dropped by the British, including Beppi's uniform, which was English.

Apprentice dishes

NERVETTI DI VITELLO

This salad (literally 'nerves of veal') was the first thing I learnt to make when I started working at the Doria Hotel in Milan at the age of fourteen. Ask your butcher for knuckles of veal (or pork or beef—you basically want the muscles and tendons that are around the knees of the animal), then simmer them with bay leaves, onions, whole tomatoes, carrots and celery for 1½ hours. Let the meat cool in the stock, then take it out. Cut off the sinews and other meat, discard the bone, and slice the meat into smaller pieces (keeping the stock for soup later on). Mix the pieces of meat with finely sliced onions, celery leaves, a few chopped capers, salt and pepper, some chilli, olive oil and a splash of vinegar. This is best served the next day so the flavours can develop— and you can keep this dish in the fridge for up to one week. The combination with the celery leaves and chopped heart of celery is fantastic, especially with crusty bread.

Note: The stock with onion and celery is good for vegetable soup or risotto.

ZUPPA PAVESE

The owner of the Doria came from Pavia, so he served the soup of his area, an egg soup. For this you need a clear chicken stock (see chapter 1). Bring it to the boil and add some finely chopped celery leaves. Melt some butter in a frying pan and gently fry a slice of bread on each side for each person you are serving. When the bread absorbs the butter and becomes crisp, put a slice in each soup bowl. Make a hollow in the middle of the bread (using the back of a spoon). Break an egg into the hollow of each slice of bread (this will keep it in place), sprinkle with parmesan, and then pour the boiling, seasoned stock over each egg. Sprinkle with more parmesan cheese, or a slice of asiago cheese, and serve.

STRACOTTO

This stew is another dish I learnt to cook at the Doria, and it's an excellent way to cook a big piece of beef rump, because the long simmering will tenderise the toughest meat. 'Stracotto' literally means overcooked. For six people you need a piece weighing about 2 kg. Don't trim the meat of fat or sinew or anything; this will all break down with the long cooking and make it very tasty.

Put some chopped onions, garlic, carrots, celery, bay leaves, the meat and 2 litres of red wine into a big container. Add rosemary, thyme, sage, chilli and whole cloves—whatever you like or have in your garden or cupboard. Leave in the refrigerator, or a cool place, for a day, then remove the meat from the marinade, drain it well then pat it dry and dust it all over with flour. Heat some chopped pancetta in oil in a large saucepan, add the meat and brown it all over. Add the marinade and some stock, then slowly simmer the whole thing for 3 hours with the lid on, leaving a tiny gap for steam to escape (you could leave a ladle in the pot, so the lid is slightly raised). Turn the meat over occasionally so it cooks evenly. Now remove the meat and cover it, keeping it in a warm place. Strain the vegetables from the liquid and chop into very small pieces, then put back in the pot and keep cooking the sauce base until it has reduced and thickened—it will concentrate into a rich sauce. Add salt and pepper to taste. Slice the meat—about 4 slices per person— then serve with mashed potatoes or soft polenta and the sauce on top.

RISOTTO CON QUAGLIE

This is another recipe I learnt early on, quail risotto. Bone 2 quails for each person who will be eating the risotto—this is a dish for four people. Toss the bones into 1 litre of simmering chicken stock. Cut the meat into small pieces.

Cook finely sliced onion and celery in butter with a pinch of grated nutmeg for about 5 minutes, until golden. Put in the quail meat, some finely chopped pancetta, 3 chopped sage leaves, a dash of white wine, some chilli and 1 teaspoonful of tomato paste, and cook for another 5 minutes. The wine should completely evaporate. Slowly add 1 teacup of rice per person, and fry it for 2 minutes, stirring constantly. Add a handful of finely chopped parsley.

Now start adding the boiling stock a little at a time to the rice (the stock must be boiling or you will interrupt the cooking of the rice), stirring until the stock is absorbed. Keep adding stock for about 20 minutes—maybe a bit less—and stirring it through, until the rice is *al dente* and moist. Next the rice has to be *mantecato* (whipped up)—throw in a lump of butter and 3 tablespoons of grated parmesan cheese, taste to see if it needs more salt and pepper, and stir vigorously for about 1 minute, until it's soft and gluey. Serve with more parmesan.

Rice in general

You can make risotto from any flavour base. For the rice I prefer arborio, not carnaroli or vialone nano, which are fashionable now. A general rule is that the wine or tomato base must be very reduced before you add the rice. If making a seafood risotto, you can flavour it with olive oil, garlic, capers, tarragon, parsley or chopped celery leaves, saffron, a little tomato or tomato paste, chives, dill, spring onion, leek or fennel seeds—*mantecato* with butter only though, no cheese.

For meat risottos you can use chicken, rabbit, minced beef or pork, pigeon, game, duck, turkey or lamb. For your base sauce with meat use onion, garlic, chopped celery, minced carrot, tomato or tomato paste mixed with wine, bay leaves, rosemary, marjoram, oregano, basil, thyme or sage. Use a good chicken or beef stock and *mantecato* with soft butter and cheese, and a little chilli at the end if needed. Without the tomato, we call this dish *in bianco*.

COTOLETTA MILANESE

For these crumbed cutlets you need 1 veal cutlet (about 250 g) per person. Trim off any sinews. With a thin sharp knife, slice along the bone to separate the meat and the bone, but don't cut all the way along—the meat should still be attached at each end. This will let the heat reach all parts of the meat evenly.

Using a wooden mallet, flatten the meat until it is just less than 1 cm thick. In a bowl, beat 3 eggs with some salt and pepper and chopped sage. In another bowl, mix dried breadcrumbs, salt and pepper, a little oregano and a little grated parmesan cheese. Toss each cutlet in flour, dip it in the egg and then coat it well with the breadcrumb mix. Now heat some butter in a frying pan, put in the cutlets, and cook each side on a low heat for about 3 or 4 minutes. You need quite a bit of butter to cook the cutlets because the breadcrumbs absorb it, and you need to cook them very slowly otherwise the crumbs will burn and the meat inside won't be cooked. When you turn the cutlets in the pan you can add some slices of lemon and cook these with the cutlets—the flavour goes through the meat and it helps to cut the grease flavour. Serve with mashed potato (which these days I like to boost with a teaspoon of truffle paste).

Camp food

In the concentration camp they didn't have a menu—when you came back from a day working, you queued up with your bowl and didn't dare complain about whatever was in the big pot in front of you. In the morning we got a slice of brown bread, occasionally spread with lard and salt. At the factory we got dumplings for lunch. At dinner it was usually boiled cabbage, peas or soup.

I guess these are something like the recipes they used ...

PEA SOUP

Soak some dried peas overnight in a big pot, then add minced onions, chopped potatoes, salt and pepper and a lot more water, then boil for 2 hours, or until the prisoners start queuing up. This soup did fill our bellies, but if I was making it these days I would boil some pork bones and bay leaves with it to give more flavour. You could also add chopped pancetta and finely sliced celery and use chicken stock instead of water.

STANGRIC

This dish bears a resemblance to Irish stew without the tomato and mutton. It was their name for a kind of stew made with off-cuts of animals (pork mostly), cabbage, potatoes and water. Apparently they just boiled them together. Sometimes they added pumpkin, or chopped sugar beets, which made it semi-sweet, and which were farmed a lot around Vienna. It's not a dish I'm nostalgic about.

DUMPLINGS

We had these sometimes with the stangric, or sweetened as a dessert. My guess is they chopped up lard or dripping into small pieces, and mixed it with flour, salt and a little water, then rolled the mixture into solid lumps, about the size of tennis balls. They boiled the dumplings in salted water for about 5 minutes. Sometimes they served them with a brown gravy; I don't know where the colour came from. The flavour would be improved if you boiled the dumplings in chicken stock, but they never used that in the camp.

If they were using the dumplings as a dessert, they would put minced sugar beet with the flour, and make a yellow sauce with more minced sugar beet.

Mountain meals

MINESTRA DI MONTAGNA

This was our best meal when I was with the partisans on top of the mountain— mountain beef soup. First get a cow, and take it up to your encampment at night, avoiding any main tracks (this step is important because if you don't follow it, you may not live to eat the meal). Don't try this with a pig, because it will be too noisy.

When you reach the camp (after 3 hours of walking through the night), put a bullet through the cow's head, tie a rope around its back ankles and hoist it over a thick tree branch so the head is about 1 metre from the ground. With a sharp knife slowly cut downwards through the middle, removing the innards and throwing the inedible bits into the bush a good distance from the camp. Keep the tripe (wash it well and keep it in salted water for 24 hours), the liver, the heart and the kidneys and put them in copper pots with salted water for cooking later. Skin the animal and cut off the best pieces of meat to barbecue on a spit over the fire. You may want to peg out the skin on the ground to dry, so you can use it as a blanket.

Chop up the rest of the cow and throw the pieces of meat and bones into a big pot with potatoes, pumpkin, chopped onions, garlic and beans and whatever herbs or mushrooms you can find growing wild in the hills or in the gardens of the shepherds who live there in peacetime. Add tomato paste if you have been able to get some from kindly shopkeepers in the valley. Cook for 3 hours or until the meat is cooked. Sometimes it tasted pretty good, depending on what ingredients you were able to find in the mountain. If it didn't taste good enough, we would add more salt and pepper; although the boiled meat was always very good.

CHAPTER THREE

CLIMBING THE LADDER IN ITALY'S GREAT HOTELS

THE TIMES
1946

ITALY WAS EMERGING FROM ITS DISASTROUS EXPERIMENT WITH FASCISM AND IN 1946 AN ELECTION HAD ABOLISHED THE MONARCHY IN FAVOUR OF A REPUBLIC. DURING THIS PERIOD THE CHRISTIAN DEMOCRATS DOMINATED ITALIAN POLITICS WITH THE ANTI-FASCIST POLITICIAN ALCIDE DE GASPERI BECOMING PRIME MINISTER IN 1946. IN 1947, A NEW CONSTITUTION WAS ADOPTED.

In 1948, the United Nations held its first meeting. Columbia released the first long playing record—33⅓ RPM as opposed to the old 78 RPM.

Roberto Rossellini's film *Rome, Open City*, a neo-realist ode to the Italian wartime resistance, offered its own resistance to all-powerful Hollywood in 1948. This period also saw Italy's emergence as a world leader in design, engineering, fashion and popular culture. The world was beginning to take notice of names like Olivetti, Lambretta, Fiat, Loren, Mastroianni and Fellini, who years later gave us the 'paparazzi'. This word was derived from a character, Paparazzo, in the Fellini film *La Dolce Vita*. An early symbol of Italian innovation and design was that of the Vespa (the name means wasp) which first appeared on Italian streets in 1946.

Right, clockwise from top: Beppi's identity card (cover); Beppi (bottom left) with army athletics corps teammates in 1948; an army portrait of Beppi; Beppi's identity card (inside).

REPVBBLICA ITALIANA

COMVNE DI

CARTA D'IDENTITA'

N°. 21.824.323

DEL SIGNOR

Polese Giuseppe

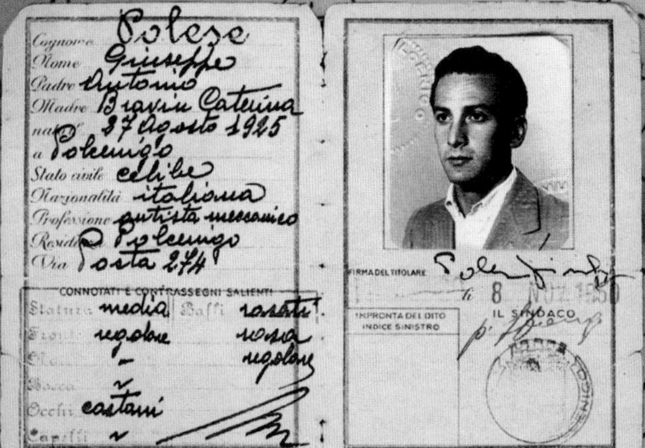
Cognome Polese

Nome Giuseppe

Padre Antonio

Madre Bravin Caterina

nato il 27 Agosto 1925

a Polcenigo

Stato civile celibe

Nazionalità italiana

Professione autista meccanico

Residenza Polcenigo

Via Posta 274

CONNOTATI E CONTRASSEGNI SALIENTI

Statura media Baffi rasati

Fronte regolare rosea

regolare

Bocca

Occhi castani

Capelli

FIRMA DEL TITOLARE

li 8 NOV. 1950

IL SINDACO

IMPRONTA DEL DITO INDICE SINISTRO

Resumed. An interrupted career

In the spring of 1945, the twenty-year-old Beppi Polese arrived in Venice on a bicycle. He had survived the labour camps of Germany and his time in the mountains with the partisans. All he wanted to do was get back to work.

He caught a *vaporetto* (ferry) across the Gulf of Venice to the Lido—a small island off Venice—and landed a job as a commis—his pre-war rank—at the Regina Hotel, then occupied by the American Red Cross. 'They gave me a job straight away because the director of the company was a Polese—no relation, but a Polese.'

Beppi stayed on the Lido for two years, first with the Regina, and then he was transferred to the Palazzo Balneare, the bathing palace, which held all the home comforts needed by the American army to survive this tough overseas posting.

> I was lodged there, and I was the one who looked after everything—
> I worked in shorts, not as a waiter. They had a big room full of
> ping pong tables—I became pretty good at ping pong—they had cases
> of Coca Cola, everything.

Ironically, in 1947, after all he had been through in the war, Beppi was called up for National Service. But Beppi adapts and survives. Remembering his time working as a boy in the bicycle shop in Polcenigo, 'when the army asked me what I could do, I told them I was a mechanic—so they sent me to Cichignola military camp south of Rome for six months and taught me to work as a mechanic and drive heavy vehicles'. Although it's interesting to speculate on the loss to Sydney's food if he had decided to continue in this direction, it's hard to imagine Beppi Polese running a garage.

After two years, he was discharged and returned to San Giovanni to regroup before throwing himself back into the luxury hotel circuit in Venice, Florence, Rome and Switzerland. First, he went back to Venice for the season, then to the Baglioni in Florence.

Beppi (left) with other waiting staff from the Excelsior Hotel in Venice where he worked as a chef de rang.

After finishing the season in Venice I went back to San Giovanni for the winter. Then, in 1948, I wrote away to the Baglioni in Florence, and they wrote back that I had a job.

The Baglioni is near the Santa Maria Novella railway station. I arrived and tried to get into the hotel by the side door—staff never go in through the front door. They stopped me and said, 'You can't come in, there's a strike on'. I said, 'Listen, I have no money, and nowhere to stay'. So the man at the hotel sent me to the union office and told me they'd give me a meal and find some accommodation. Even though I didn't belong to the union, when I got there the office secretary gave me the money for a meal, but told me there was nowhere for me to stay. I went back to the hotel, and spoke to the head waiter. He said, 'Okay, you can sleep here', and he sent me up to the staff rooms in the attic. He also allowed me to work against the union's wishes.

One of the really difficult things about seasonal work at that time was that every time you went to a new town to work, you had to get a resident's permit which cost 30,000 lire. This applied in Rome, Milan and Florence but not in Venice—I guess because I came from Friuli, which was in the same region.

We would work seven days a week in the season. We'd serve breakfast, then prepare for lunch and serve lunch until 3 o'clock, and then we got a couple of hours off until 5.30 when we'd go back and start preparing for dinner and work until 11.30 pm.

Sometimes during those hours off I'd rent a bicycle and ride in the Cascine Park along the Arno River. I often went with a friend who was the second head waiter, Carlo Zambon, who came from a village near San Giovanni. We'd also go to Piazza della Signoria where there was a spaghetti bar (not to mention Michelangelo's *David*) where we'd eat the spaghetti standing up—it was fantastic, like Harry's Café de Wheels (the famous pie shop down by the wharfs in Sydney). And sometimes we'd take out the tourist girls—guests of the hotel, American, Dutch. Was it allowed? We never asked. If the girl was happy to come out, why not?

A couple of months after I started at the Baglioni, I was walking around the shops near Santa Maria Novella and I saw this shirt, and I liked it very much. But I still had no money. Every afternoon I would go and look at this shirt, and then at the end of the month I bought it. It felt so good.

In 1950, Beppi worked for a time in a nightclub off the Via Veneto, called Rupe d'Arpea and Fiametto. This was the beginnings of the era portrayed by Federico Fellini in his 1960 film, *La Dolce Vita*, although at that early stage it was still a relatively tame scene. There was no striptease on a table like that executed by the actress Aichée Nanà at the Rugantino in Rome in 1958, an event recreated in *La Dolce Vita*. The patrons of the Rupe d'Arpea were circumspect by contrast— if a little tight-fisted.

> It was very elegant. There was a floor show, there were dancing girls. But there were problems. Many of the patrons were the *nobile*, the gilded youth, they had titles—the Prince of Rome, the Count of Rome and so on—but that's all they had. They came to the club, but they didn't pay and they didn't tip. Downstairs from the club was the Fiametta—here they played first-run movies. From here, I went back to the Baglioni and that's when they promoted me to demi chef.

The rungs on the ladder

In the world of the grand hotels in which Beppi Polese worked, waiting was a profession, a profession with, like any other, a hierarchy of skills and status. You began as an apprentice, and, depending on your skill and dedication, ascended to the giddy heights of head waiter—a position of great prestige.

It was at the Grand Hotel Baglioni in Florence, formerly the home of the Bertolini princes, in its famous roof garden overlooking the city, that Beppi Polese was given an important, if humiliating, lesson in getting it right.

> In the roof garden of the Baglioni I learnt how to dissect a fish. I was twenty-four, and I had just been promoted from commis to demi chef.
>
> Every grand hotel had a big table with varieties of seafood and *antipasti* on display (today, a smaller version of just such a fresh produce display is to be seen

at the entrance to Beppi's). In summer they have big salmon, which they steam with lemon, celery, onion, salt and pepper, and bay leaves. They make different sauces—mayonnaise with a bit of mustard, horseradish, lemon and butter sauce, which they put in little jugs, called *sauciers*, next to the fish.

The salmon looks beautiful with the skin removed, decorated with lemon and parsley. The way to serve it is to go along the bones, slice diagonally and lift off the flesh to a separate plate.

The first time I did this, I cut it across, not in line with the grain. So it made a mess. The pieces crumbled and the presentation didn't look nice. The head waiter, Angelo Bravin, said, 'You're a barbarian!' We were about twenty waiters and Bravin called them all around to watch what he was saying to me. He was embarrassing me in front of other members of the staff because he had promoted me, and if he didn't punish me he would lose his strength. Head waiters are sure of themselves. Nobody can correct them. The behaviour in the dining room has to be impeccable. The head waiter judges you. Nobody can afford to do anything wrong. Or you never work in the city again.

I respected him and I appreciated that the man gave me a job. We didn't have the luxury to judge head waiters as people. My responsibility was to prove to him that he had made the right choice in promoting me. He wasn't shouting, just talking to everybody, showing me up in front of them. It was a lesson for everyone.

He had promoted me from commis to demi chef because he saw the way I worked. I was fast, I did things right, served up to sixteen people on my own. Everybody can do the job but not everybody can do it properly. The head waiter notices everything that goes on. Your status depends on the head waiter's decision, and once he promotes you, that is written on your résumé. Any places you go, they trust the judgment of your last head waiter. It says you are qualified, and it doesn't matter if you're in Venice, Rome or Florence, it proves you've got the experience. The hotel business, the restaurant business, is controlled by résumés. The title was given to me by the head waiter and the head waiter is the king of the dining room. But nobody had taught me how to cut the salmon. You were expected to know because you were supposed to watch how the others did it. My time was very tough.

When you work in our game, you take the opportunity if the opportunity is there. You learn to be quick, and smart. Once it is embedded in your bones, you become a good waiter.

In the winter, the wages were much higher—about 100,000 lire a month—but there were no tips. During the season, the basic wage was around 20,000 lire a month by agreement with the union. Service of 12.5 per cent was added automatically to the bill. We shared that, according to our rank, on a point system we called 'the trunk'. For example, an apprentice gets 2 points, a demi chef 4 to 6 depending on experience, and a head waiter 16. In some places it was abused—in one place I worked the girl who walked the dog got 2 points. But our personal tips we kept. When I worked the last season at the Excelsior in Venice before coming to Australia, I earned enough in wages and tips—around 200,000 to 280,000 lire—to pay for the trip. This is how the ranks work, and the duties of each rank:

Apprentice: You would stay in this rank usually for one or two years, until you proved yourself. You do all the dirty work—preparing the *mise en place*—making sure the crockery, the cutlery and the glasses are correctly stored in the servery, setting the table and cleaning and dusting in the morning. I did this in the Albergo Doria for one year.

Commis: Tells the apprentice what to do, sets the table, picks up dockets from the chef de rang, takes them to the kitchen and places the order, then brings the dishes out when the time comes. The commis has the responsibility of serving the dishes that the chef de rang assembles or cooks on the *guéridon*.

The *guéridon* is a small table on wheels placed next to the customer's table and food is served onto plates from this trolley. The food is brought from the kitchen in a salver (a covered metal tray) by the commis and the chef de rang removes the lid. He either serves, dissects or cooks the food at the *guéridon*. Examples of *guéridon* cooking include veal, breast of chicken, *filet mignon en boîte* and *crêpes Suzette*.

The commis is an assistant to the chef de rang. Once the chef de rang plates the dish, the commis serves it to the diner, from the left. It's here you

learn to do things in a nice way, a respectful way—you can't be rough. The commis also pulls out the chairs for the customer and places the napkins on their laps.

I was commis at the Al Corso in Milan for about eighteen months, then at the Gritti Palace in Venice for eight months until I went to Vienna. I stayed a commis through various other jobs and events until 1950.

Chef de rang: Responsible for six tables, seats the customer and answers questions. The chef de rang must know the principles of serving—each person has to be asked about the vegetables which are always served separately, and salad which is always served on the side—it is a sacrilege to put hot food and cold food together on the same plate.

As well as learning to cut a salmon along the spine, I learnt not to serve spinach with fish. When you're serving a *bistecca fiorentina* (Florentine steak), you have to cut the bone out, trim the fat and slice it for the customer. And you must pick up a little juice from the hollow in the wooden plate it arrives on and spoon a little juice over the meat. Another skill is the peeling and dissecting of fruit according to a prescribed system for each kind of fruit. The fruit must never be touched by hand, and must be delivered to the customer ready to be eaten.

Demi chef: The same duties as the chef de rang—you have your own commis—except you are only given five tables and usually in the worst section of the dining room. You serve the tourists, you don't get the high class people.

Drinks waiter: Takes the drinks order, hands out the wine list. He uses the commis of the chef de rang. (The barman has his own commis behind the bar.)

Second head waiter: Depends on the grade of the restaurant. The Excelsior (on the Lido) had first head waiter, second and third head waiter. He walks around and supervises every section. If he sees a fork missing, he'll tell the chef de rang who will tell the commis. It's a chain of command like the army. The second takes customers to their table, and hands them over to the chef de rang.

Sommelier: Takes wine orders, advises on wine choices and serves the wine, tasting it beforehand.

Head waiter: Knows everybody, the top person in the dining room, and has the responsibility for the entire room for all meals, as well as the nightclub if there is one. The knowledge of a good head waiter is magnificent. They know their staff and they know their customers—their habits, their food and how they like it served. For example, a chef de rang may have ten people in his section. The head waiter would say, 'This gentleman likes his food this way, the other likes it that way'. He would know the preferences of everybody in the party.

There was a famous head waiter at the time, Lo Di Gianni, who worked at the Grand Hotel in Rome. He had his own staff, his own *brigata*. In the summer he would go to Venice with that *brigata* and work at a hotel there. A lot of the customers he knew in Rome would come to him in Venice. They followed the head waiter.

This is how the system worked in Italy. The first person the customer saw on entering the restaurant was the head waiter at the desk, who greeted them and checked the booking. The second head waiter took the customers to the table, and passed them on to the chef de rang. The chef de rang handed out menus, and asked if they had any special needs. French dishes were written in French, no translation. The people who went to these six or seven star hotels travel internationally. And anyway, the chef de rang is there to explain. He then leaves them and the drinks waiter comes along, leaves the wine list and takes drink orders. The chef de rang then comes back to take the order, which he gives to the commis who goes to the kitchen to give the order, followed by the apprentice. When the dishes are ready, the commis brings them out to the *guéridon*.

The chef de rang prepares the pasta at the table, saying, 'Signora va bene cosi?' (Madame is feeling well today); 'Salsa sopra?' (sauce on top?); 'Po di formagio?' (a little cheese?); 'Pepe?' (pepper?). While the chef de rang mixes the food and puts it on the plate, he directs the commis to take it to the customer.

The chef de rang never corrects the commis in front of the customer. Only afterwards. The customer picks up the wine with the right hand, so the waiter must serve the plate from the left. Or when you do silver service, going round with the tray, you must be on the left side. Be close to the plate so as not to drop it on the tablecloth. You must never serve across the customer. The word silver service is only used in Australia and America. In Italy it's called 'table d'hôte' or 'guéridon'.

The customer doesn't talk to the commis because the chef de rang is always there, he's at his station. He writes the dockets. The commis comes and goes to the kitchen and the apprentice follows, learning the skills to get upgraded to commis level. The second head waiter supervises every section.

The head waiter can answer any question about anything whatsoever. The head waiter does the roster, and could have up to forty waiters working at different grades. Some waiters specialised in room service. Breakfast 6 to 10 am, then one hour rest. Then lunch, then rest, then dinner, then, as at the Excelsior nightclub, until midnight. You may have one day off a week, but in the peak season you may keep working. The union only worries about the basic wages. You are free to work as much as you like.

After working in such a fantastic system, coming to Australia was a shock. There was nothing like the system I was used to. I was confused. For example, in Italy the food was 50 per cent French and 50 per cent Italian—although when I left, there were more Italian dishes coming onto the menu. In Australia, it was all French, but it was a different kind of French, dishes I'd never seen or served—cooked by an Egyptian chef in one place—I was truly lost. I'd never heard of steak Diane, but I had to cook it on the *guéridon*.

THE TIMES
1950

AS BEPPI BEGAN TO THINK ABOUT LEAVING, ITALY PREPARED FOR WHAT WAS EVENTUALLY TO BE KNOWN AS THE ITALIAN ECONOMIC MIRACLE OF THE 1950S. ORDINARY ITALIANS BEGAN TO PROSPER IN SPITE OF FREQUENT LABOUR UNREST AND STRIKES KNOWN AS THE ITALIAN DISEASE. BECAUSE OF THESE PROBLEMS AND UNAWARE OF THE COMING BOOM, MILLIONS OF ITALIANS MIGRATED TO AMERICA, SWITZERLAND, ARGENTINA AND AUSTRALIA.

This halfway point in the twentieth century also saw the beginning of the Korean War and the signing of the Sino-Soviet Friendship Treaty: the beginnings of The Cold War.

Above: After a few years in various top Italian restaurants, Beppi became disenchanted with the seasonal demands of the industry, and began to think about finding more steady work abroad.

Looking abroad

At the end of 1950 Beppi had begun to grow tired of the season on, season off, method of working. He applied for a job at the Savoy in London—where he might have learnt about steak Diane—but his passport took so long to arrive, the job lapsed. He began to think about Australia.

At that time in my area, men would go out and work all over Europe in hotels and restaurants during the season. Then when they retired, they would buy a block of land and open a restaurant. In my time we didn't have any local business. The only way we could work was to go out and work seasonally. In the winter, the men came home and played cards and drank grappa. Now there are shoe factories, furniture factories—people have a reason to stay. Back then I had no reason to stay. I wanted to go somewhere where I could work.

A year before, in the winter, I was talking to my mother about Toni de Fort and she said, 'Why don't you write to him and see if there's any work in Australia?' I remembered my father had been in Australia. I sent Toni all the documentation and asked if it was possible to sponsor me. I didn't know if there was work in Australia but I took the chance. He wrote back and said he would try. And I wrote to the Department of Immigration. About a year later I finally heard back from them. I had to go to the consulate in Venice to present myself. January 1951. I had to have an X-ray—you had to be in perfect health to be allowed into Australia.

I'd accepted a job at the Excelsior on the Lido starting in February for the summer—when you start the season, first you have to open up the hotel, clean all the silver and so on and prepare for the season ahead. While I was working, the consulate asked me to go for another X-ray. You see, in winter in San Giovanni, we ride our motorbikes, and I had caught bronchitis, so they had to check that my chest was clear. I went and it was okay and I got the permit to come to Australia.

Before I left I spoke to my old friend Carlo Cipollato who was the head waiter working with me at the Gritti Palace at the time. When I told him about my application, he told me about his brother, Guido, who had been sponsored by a restaurant in Melbourne, Marios, in 1949. He gave me his address (he now owned his own restaurant, the Venezia) and I promised to get in touch.

I finished the season at the Excelsior in September, 1952. I booked a trip on the *Neptunia*, which was due to leave the following month, arriving in Australia in November.

It was very sad to be leaving my mother and father, and when I said goodbye to them in San Giovanni I cried. We lived about 100 metres from the bus stop, and while I was packing, my parents watched with long faces. Then we went to the bus stop and waited. I can't explain the sadness I felt. It was so strange, so difficult—the uncertainty of leaving your mother and father, and of not knowing where you were going, so far away. My father did it, and thinking of his experience would have scared me off ...

My brother and aunt Gina were in Genoa where I'd pick up the ship. I remember they took me out for something to eat. And then on the boat when the ship left I cried again, watching my brother and aunt in the distance. You know, we were a very poor family. My mother and father worked very hard to feed the five children. In that kind of life you go out every day with such uncertainty, and every day you have the problem of getting enough food to survive. You grow up with fear. To go away and leave your family, you can imagine the feelings I had. Feelings of sadness and fear, not knowing what I would find on the other side of the world.

Right: Beppi in Switzerland, where he worked as a waiter for a time prior to making the decision to move to Australia.

Fine dining

PESCE IN SAOR

This is a famous antipasto from Venice. You use fillets of fish—garfish, John Dory or sardines are good—about 200 g per person, but be sure to remove all bones. Toss the fillets in flour and fry them in oil for 2 or 3 minutes, until crisp. Take out the fish and place them in a single layer in a baking dish. Add fresh oil to the pan, 6 sliced onions, a few sage and bay leaves, and cook for at least 5 minutes or until soft. Add salt and pepper.

Put in 2 soupspoons of sultanas, 1 teaspoon of chilli flakes or peppercorns, 1½ cups of white wine vinegar, 1 glass of white wine and some water, and simmer for 10 minutes. Add pine nuts (you can toast them beforehand for a nuttier taste). Pour the sauce over the fish, let it cool and then put it in the fridge. You can serve this any time over the next week with finely grated carrots.

Note: To keep the white colour of the onion, squeeze the juice of ½ lemon over them 10 minutes before cooking.

FEGATO ALLA VENEZIANA

This is a classic from Venice, very simple to make, but only if you like liver. Mostly you use calf's liver, but you could use pork if you enjoy a stronger flavour.

Peel the skin off the liver, clean out any nasty bits and cut it into paper-thin slices about 10-cm wide.

Cook some finely sliced onion in butter until it softens and starts to sweeten and turn light golden (at least 5 minutes). Add some sage leaves (or rosemary if you prefer) and the pieces of liver. Add some salt and pepper and chilli.

Turn the heat up high and sauté, stirring continuously for 1 minute so the liver pieces don't get tough and dry. Add some parsley. Keep stirring so the onion doesn't burn. Serve with polenta, either soft or grilled (see chapter 1).

FETTUCCINE AL ALFREDO

This is a simple but rich Roman dish that depends on the quality of the pasta, so if you can possibly make it yourself it is better (see my mother's recipe in chapter 1). Make a sauce by whisking a large dob of butter, ½ teacup of cream and a sprinkle of nutmeg in a large frying pan and stir continuously for 10 minutes or until it reduces and thickens. Meanwhile, boil the fettuccine (for no more than 2 minutes if it's fresh).

When the fettuccine is almost cooked, drain it and toss it into the cream sauce. Keep it on a low heat for 10 minutes, tossing it and adding a little of the pasta water if the sauce gets too thick, then stir ½ cup of grated parmesan through it. Season with salt and pepper and serve straight away.

WHOLE FISH

Italians prefer their fish served whole as it has better flavour when cooked on the bone, and good waiters know how to dissect it in front of the customer. Snapper or silver bream—or any small fish on the bone (about 350 g for each person)—is ideal for this presentation.

Usually the fish has already been gutted and scaled at the shop, but if it hasn't, get a sharp knife and scrape along the skin, going against the grain of the scales upward toward the head. The scales should lift off easily. Then slice through the belly and remove the guts. Rinse the fish out then put a little salt, pepper and lemon inside. Now carve an S-shaped groove into one side of the fish, along the ribs from near the head, down to the tail. Sprinkle in some salt and squeeze lemon juice into the groove, so it penetrates. You can put a little tarragon in the cut too, if you like it, or even chilli—or any flavour that you prefer.

Dry the fish and lightly coat it in flour so it won't stick to the pan, then warm some oil in a big frying pan, not too hot. Lay the fish in the pan with the non-cut

side facing down. Cover the pan with a lid and cook over a low flame—so the heat can penetrate to the bone without burning the skin. Cook for 5 minutes, until that side is brown. The steam will help dissolve the salt on the top side and let it penetrate. Turn the fish and cook for another 5 minutes. Lift it out onto a big plate.

To fillet the fish you need a fish knife, a fork and two (more) plates (one for the flesh and one for the bones). Cut under the gill to remove the side fin (the wing) and its bone. With the fork, pull away any fins at the top of the spine or under the belly. Now find where the head is connected to the body, slide the knife in and slice along the bones towards the tail, so the fillet is separated. Put the fillet on a separate plate. Lift off the stomach (*la ventresca*, my favourite part) and any more flesh and separate any loose bones. Holding the tail, lift the skeleton and head away from the flesh on the bottom half and put that on the rubbish plate (it's not wise to turn the fish over, because you risk breaking the fillet).

Now go over the flesh, scraping away any bones that are left.

Some people don't want the skin—myself I love it—so you ask them about the skin as you fillet the fish.

Now dress the fillets with lemon and olive oil. You don't squeeze the lemon in case it squirts the customer. Instead stab it with a fork and drizzle the juice over the flesh. Use more oil than lemon plus salt and freshly ground black pepper.

CRESPELLE WITH STRAWBERRY AND ORANGE LIQUEUR

Many of the dishes served in the great hotels of Italy are designed to provide a theatrical experience. We used to (and still do) flame the *crespelle* (crêpes) in front of the customer. The kitchen made the *crespelle*, and the waiters finished the sauce at the table by adding the orange liqueur and flaming it. When you are making it at home, you need to cook this dish using a gas cooktop. You can't flame it if you are using an electric one.

Make the batter by mixing 100 g of flour with 2 eggs and a pinch of salt, and slowly adding 50 ml of orange juice, 3 dessertspoonfuls of caster sugar and 200 ml of milk. As you're beating in the milk, you judge when the mixture has reached the right consistency—not too thick and not too runny. Warm a frying pan, finely coat it with butter or oil, and pour on just enough batter to spread thinly over the pan as you tilt it. Over low heat, cook for about 3 minutes until the underside is golden, flip it over and cook the second side for about 2 minutes. From this mixture you should be able to make about 12 *crespelle*.

Now the sauce: melt about 100 g of butter in a frying pan and stir in 100 g of sugar, a cinnamon stick, the zest of 1 orange, and 50 ml of orange juice. Simmer for a couple of minutes to reduce the liquid and dissolve the sugar, then gently place 2 crespelle per diner into the pan, put a strawberry in the middle, fold into a triangle, splash in some sweet orange liqueur (Cointreau or Grand Marnier according to your taste) and tilt the pan so the liqueur runs to the edge and catches fire from the flame. Allow the alcohol mixture to reduce for 1–2 minutes, then serve, pouring the sauce on top and sprinking with some caster sugar.

If you want to make *crêpes alle fragole* instead, put sliced strawberries into the sauce along with the pancakes, and splash in Galliano as the liqueur to be flamed. Stir in a little cream at the end of the simmering process.

Street food

LA SPAGHETTATA

Late at night in Florence after work at the Baglioni Hotel, the staff would go to a stall called La Spaghettata near Piazza Signoria and eat pasta standing up. The stall offered a wide variety of sauces, and a big pot of boiling water on one side for the spaghetti. Gulping a quick bowl late at night is known as a 'spaghettata', which we might translate as a 'pasta snack'. These are a few ideas for sauces ...

Al burro e formaggio (butter and cheese): Melt a dob of butter in a frying pan with some chopped sage and celery leaves, nutmeg and salt and pepper. Add boiled spaghetti, stir so the spaghetti absorbs the butter, add a handful of grated parmesan and serve.

Pizzaiola: Fry some onion, garlic and pancetta in butter for 5 minutes. Add a sprinkle of oregano, 4 chopped tomatoes (or 1 tin of tomatoes) and 1 teaspoon of tomato paste. Simmer for 15 minutes. Throw in some cooked spaghetti and stir for 2 to 3 minutes so the pasta absorbs the flavours, then serve.

Puttanesca: Fry some garlic in oil with 3 crushed anchovy fillets and a bit of chilli if you like it. Add a handful of capers, 1 cup of black olives (seeds removed), chopped parsley (or celery leaves if you prefer them as I do) and 4 chopped tomatoes (or 1 tin of tomatoes). Simmer for 10 minutes, add the spaghetti, and stir for another 2 or 3 minutes, then serve.

Aglio olio prezzemolo con acciughe e peperoncino: The name of this sauce in English is garlic oil with parsley and chilli pepper. Fry some sliced garlic, chilli, 3 crushed anchovies and parsley in a fair bit of olive oil (a generous soupspoon of oil for each person eating). You can add capers if you like. After 2 minutes, add the boiled spaghetti, which you coat with the ingredients in the pan and stir for another 2 to 3 minutes. Serve with ground pepper or chilli.

Al prosciutto: Heat some butter in a large frying pan, add some chopped garlic, finely chopped prosciutto, celery leaves, 1 tomato (chopped) then cook for 5 minutes. Add a splash of white wine, reduce, then a splash of cream. Simmer for 2 minutes to reduce, then add the spaghetti and stir for 2 to 3 minutes before serving.

CHAPTER FOUR

ARRIVAL IN A STRANGE NEW LAND

Left: Despite the sparkling harbour and majestic Harbour Bridge, Beppi's first impressions of his new home, Sydney, were not very favourable—scorching hot weather and scruffy houses with galvanised roofs ...

THE TIMES
1952

IN FEBRUARY 1953, GEORGE VI DIED. HIS DAUGHTER ELIZABETH QUEEN OF AUSTRALIA AND GREAT BRITAIN ASCENDED TO THE THRONE. THE UNITED STATES EXPLODED ITS FIRST THERMONUCLEAR 'HYDROGEN' BOMB AT ENEWETAK IN THE MARSHALL ISLANDS ON 1 NOVEMBER.

In November, future Australian Prime Minister Edward Gough Whitlam was elected to the Parliament following the resignation of the seat of Werriwa by the son of an Italian migrant, Hubert Peter Lazzarini, whose father Pietro had migrated in 1849 after the fall of the Roman Republic.

Earlier that year a merino ram belonging to a Mr W Merriman won the Grand Champion ribbon at the Wool Show. Mr Merriman later attended the Peter Pan charity foundation's Wool Ball at Romano's, one of Sydney's fashionable nightclubs. Beppi would land his first job there later that year.

It was a Mad Hatter's ball and according to *The Sydney Morning Herald*, 'exotic and fascinating headdresses were worn with magnificent evening gowns … men who refused to wear "those silly things" were persuaded to buy them at the stall at the entrance to Romano's'. Australia was still riding on the sheep's back. Sheep farmers, like Mr Merriman, and wool buyers, like Marcel Dekyvere and his 'socialite' wife Nola, constituted the crème de la crème of Sydney society—a term some vicious commentators labelled an oxymoron.

An important event for Sydney food at that time was the publication of *Oh, For a French Wife* (1953) by Ted Moloney and Deke Coleman, both employees of the J Walter Thompson advertising agency. Moloney would become a great supporter of Beppi's restaurant.

At this time in the *Herald*, a flatette was advertised for rent in the Sydney nightlife district of Kings Cross for £1 a week; a 'very modern' two bedroom flat in the inner-eastern suburb of Woollahra at £6. There were no restaurants for sale in Sydney, but in Port Macquarie, on New South Wales' north coast, there was a 'high class restaurant and coffee lounge' with a small residence attached for £3000.

New land, new beginnings

The *Neptunia*, the ship that carried the twenty-seven-year-old Beppi Polese to Sydney, was one of three—the others, the *Oceania*, the *Australia* and the *Fairsea*—belonging to the Lloyd Triestino line. These ships would bring almost 200,000 migrants to Australia in the 1950s and '60s—a fraction of total immigration numbers. The *Neptunia*, decommissioned from naval war service, and departing from Genoa, took the route through the Suez Canal.

Although, by all accounts, accommodation and food were, at best, rudimentary for Beppi, it was 'a fantastic trip'—after working seven days a week from breakfast through to dinner, he did nothing for six weeks but play cards, sunbake and make friends. One particular friend was a champion ice skater returning to Sydney, Thelma Homsey. She and Beppi became close friends—he practised his English with her—and she later introduced him to her family and her boyfriend in Sydney. 'He had an MG', Beppi recalled, 'and when I saw it I said to myself, one day I'm going to have one of those'. (The car Beppi actually ended up buying was a Fiat 1100.)

The *Neptunia* arrived in Sydney via Perth, Adelaide and Melbourne, where passengers were given two days ashore. While in Melbourne, he contacted Carlo Cipollato's brother, Guido, at his restaurant, the Venezia. Guido had come to the city in 1949 with two other chefs from Italy, one of them Primo Fasetta who Beppi would later work with in Sydney, the other a Signor Magris. They had been sponsored by Mario Vigano, who had arrived in Melbourne with his wife Teresa from Milan in the 1930s (he was the grandfather of the late restaurateur Mietta O'Donnell) to work in his grand restaurant Mario's on the corner of Little Bourke and Exhibition Streets. After reading Beppi's résumés, Guido Cipollato rang his friend, the head waiter at Romano's in Sydney, one Bepi Pilotto, and they arranged for Beppi to come and see him.

In Melbourne he also caught up with Aldo Zuzza, also from San Giovanni, who had preceded Beppi to Australia by six months. There was a more than usually close connection: Aldo and his brother were both delivered into the world by Beppi's mother in her role as the village midwife.

Aldo would later work with Beppi, and then open his own restaurant in Sydney, Darcy's in Paddington. Aldo was later joined by his brother, Giuseppe (Beppino), who also eventually opened a restaurant in Sydney, The Mixing Pot in Glebe.

Beppi had picked up a menu from Mario's in Melbourne, and discovered that the dishes were both familiar and strange: he was fascinated by the way the menu mixed three languages. The 'special luncheon' dated Thursday, 27 November 1952, offered four courses for six shillings and sixpence (6s 6d). It included a vegetable soup called 'minestrone Milanese', a 'consomme Italiana', something called 'spaghetti bolognese' which turned out to be pasta with a meat sauce (which Beppi knew as a ragù). Then there was goulash ungherese, roast lamb boulangere, and desserts of ice cream, fruit salad or cheese. The 'specials cooked at your table' included steak Diane (a mystery to him) at 9s and *crêpes Suzette* at 5s. Coffee espresso was 1s and Turkish coffee was 1s 6d.

What Beppi was seeing first-hand was that strange Australian cuisine of the time known as 'Continental'—a term imported from the old country, which meant 'any food from across the Channel'. Australia embraced this description—indeed, many years later, in 1963, a photograph in *The Sunday Telegraph* of four people eating at Beppi's was captioned:

Australians make up the majority of those who enjoy continental cooking, this happy foursome at Beppi's is an example.

The Sydney that Beppi Polese first saw in November 1952 when he sailed down Sydney Harbour aboard the *Neptunia* would be hard to recognise today. About the only landmark still recognisable would be the Sydney Harbour Bridge, then in its twentieth year. The Sydney Opera House would not open until 1973, and the low-lying skyline was dominated by the radio-transmitting AWA Tower. At 111 metres, its design loosely based on the Eiffel Tower, it would remain the tallest structure in the city until the 1960s.

Although Italian migrants were beginning to arrive in their thousands, there was very little familiar food for them to eat unless they had access to a kitchen—and even then simple ingredients like pasta, tomato paste and olive oil were not easy to find.

Curiously enough, there was an Italian restaurant, more of a workman's café, La Veneziana, opened by Carlo and Angelina Lorenzi the year Beppi arrived, at 71–73 Stanley Street in East Sydney, within sight of what was to become Beppi's and minutes away from the city centre.

At home, Australians were, for the main part, eating the food of the first settlers and convicts, Anglo-Celtic dishes: roast lamb, roast beef, steak, tripe in onion sauce. You could get two kinds of potatoes—washed and unwashed—and if people ate pasta, it would have been tinned spaghetti in tomato sauce. It was the beginning of the era of frozen convenience foods—the refrigerator and the freezer soon to become as important in the home as the stove.

For most, eating out wasn't much better. With the exception of the nightclubs and the restaurants for the exclusive use of the monied classes—to which Beppi Polese would automatically gravitate—there was little on the table. Frederick Mayer, founder of the Sydney food business, F Mayer Imports, arrived from South Africa in 1950. Of the Australian restaurant scene at the time, he wrote in a memoir, 'When we first arrived in Australia … food was a real oddity. You would go to a restaurant, it would look great, clean, with white tablecloths et cetera, but all that was on the menu would be meat pies and sausage rolls'.

Beppi's first impressions of the city were not good. He was supposed to be met by his mother's cousin, Toni de Fort, who worked at Sargents Bakery, but he couldn't be seen anywhere when they docked at Woolloomooloo.

At the dock I looked around and I didn't see anybody I knew. Apparently Toni de Fort was there, but we missed each other—I was with Thelma's family. I suppose he also thought I'd arrive destitute, but no, I was very elegant. Thelma left with her parents and I was left alone on the dock.

I caught a taxi to the address I had in Alexandria [a suburb to the west of the city centre]. I looked at the terrace houses and said to myself, '*Porca*

Right: Beppi's first glimpse of Australian dining—the Mario's menu that so perplexed Beppi when he arrived.

MINIMUM CHARGE 7/-

TABLE TO FIRST

AILS Lobster   Juice 1/6
D'OEUVRES Dan   iare 12/- Hors
        Smol   d Snails 7/- Pat
        Spe   order
RS Plain Oys   /9 Devilled — Fr
  Angels on

Mario's Chef . . .
"Claudio Magris" Suggests
for Dinner . . . .
Thursday 27-11-52

Tomato Juice 1/6
Pate de Foi Gras 4/6
Lobster Cocktail 3/6
Prawns Cocktail 4/6
Sydney Rock Oysters 7/6 - 3/9

Minestrone Milanese 2/-
Cream Onions 2/-
Consomme Italiana 1/6
Ravioli Piemontese 3/3
Girellini of Veal with Gnocchi Piemontese 8/6
Piccatina with Mushrooms 9/-
Chicken Chasseur with Rice 10/-
Ham Madera Sauce 8/-
French Cutlet 8/-
Risotto alla Veneziana 7/-
Tournedos Zingara 9/6
Brains Beurre Noir 7/6
Steak Marchandeau 8/6
Filet Mignon Siron Sauce
T Bone Fiorentina 9/-
Grilled Liver Lionese 8/6
Mixed Grill Americana 8/6
Fried Whiting Colbert Sauce 9/-
Schnapper Livornese 8/6
Prawns Indiana with Rice 9/6
Lobster Mornay 9/-
Fish Salad - Cold colation 8/-
Ham Salad - Cold egg Russa 8/-
Omelette Italiana 6/6
Omelette Parmantiere 6/6
Asparagus Milanese 6/-

Fonduta of Cheese 2/6
Cream Caramel 2/-
Bavaraise Au Chocolat 2/6

OR CHOOSE FROM OUR "A LA CARTE" MENU

SPECIALS COOKED BESIDE YOUR TABLE
Spaghetti Saltati or Marinara 6/6
Steak Diane 9/-
Cheese Veneziana 3/-
Fruit Flambee 5/-
Crepe Suzette 5/-
        Coffee Espresso 1/-
        Turkish Coffee 1/6

If in Town tomorrow why not
MARIO'S SPECIAL LUNCHEON

4 COURSES		6/6
1 COURSE		4/6

OUR DINING ROOMS ARE FULLY AIR CONDITIONED FOR
YOUR COMFORT

miseria! Why did I come here?' It was very depressing. I wasn't impressed to begin with—galvanised roof houses in a city like Sydney.

I knocked on the door. A woman came out and I introduced myself. 'Oh', she said, 'my father went to the dock to welcome you! Sit here, he will come back soon'. It was nearly summer, and the building had an iron roof. I remember sitting in the backyard and it was so hot. When de Fort did come, he took me to a boarding house near Central Station in Surry Hills. Another terrace house, very squalid, and a room with two beds and a wardrobe. Then he took me to another boarding house nearby to eat lunch with some other Italian emigrants.

Two days later I went to see Bepi Pilotto at Romano's—his name was really Anastasio, he was Hungarian, but he passed himself as Italian and used the name Bepi. When I went to work there he insisted on calling me Giuseppe. I said, 'I don't mind, call me anything you want'. The second head waiter was a German, named Schmidt, and I spoke a bit of German. They asked me to come down and try out at a party for twenty people. So I went at 5 o'clock, and worked like normal. When the dinner party was over they told me I could start the next day. I mean, I knew what I was doing.

But I didn't recognise the dishes. I was very confused. And I had trouble understanding the way Australians spoke English. There was an Italian fellow, Angelo Peruch, he was working there, he helped me quite a lot. Peruch helped me with taking orders. I made a lot of mistakes. They gave me a section. They were strange dishes, mostly French—but not the French dishes I knew. Not much Italian. I found it very hard to understand the system. After a couple of months they put me in the bar, serving the pre-lunch and dinner drinks, and that was easy. They drank whiskey, brandy, cocktails like the Brandy Crusta—you'd take the order, go to the bar, get your drink and the head waiter would put it on the tab.

The owner of Romano's, Azzalin Orlando Romano, was born in 1894 at Padua in Italy, christened Romano Orlando, his original surname Azzalin. He migrated with his family to England, where he began working as a page in a hotel in Bristol, and then worked his way through the ranks, working in Nice, Monte Carlo, Paris, Berlin and Madrid before returning to England and eventually becoming a head waiter, first at London's Ritz Hotel. He spoke five languages, and claimed to have served every king in Europe.

He changed his name while working at the Ritz, and met Percy Stewart Dawson while managing the Hyde Park Hotel. Dawson brought him to Australia in 1923 to run his restaurant, The Ambassadors', in the city.

Dawson had opened The Ambassadors' as the result of an incident at the Wentworth Hotel involving a 'lady in a low-cut dress' and a 'slightly drunk party-goer'—Dawson—described in a newspaper article reporting the scuffle as a 'Sydney jeweller and well-known man about town'. He was thrown out of the hotel and vowed to open his own place from which he could never be evicted. It was the plushest place in Sydney at the time, with a ballroom for 400 and six chefs.

In 1927, Romano left The Ambassadors' and opened the first Romano's in Pitt Street in the heart of the city, then in 1938 moved it to the basement of the Prudential Insurance building in nearby Castlereagh Street. Business flourished during the war with the patronage of American officers and, it was said, the sale of unlicensed liquor. The restaurant employed a staff of eighty, there was an orchestra, concealed lighting, 138 wall mirrors and a bust of Napoleon.

Romano had a farm at Baulkham Hills, 30 kilometres north-west of the city, which supplied much of the produce. Anybody who was anybody who came to Sydney during that era—and that included everyone from wealthy sheikhs, Vivien Leigh and Maurice Chevalier—wined, dined and danced at Romano's. Fashionable young women had their photographs taken lunching there wearing extravagant hats, which were described in great detail: 'The Hat of the Week 18 May 1952— Mrs W S Bennett's black side dipped cap from which soared a huge feather pom pom, the whole enveloped in black mesh netting' (from the *Herald*).

Romano himself was an elegant figure in white tie and tails with an aquiline nose and a pencil-thin moustache, usually holding a cigar and always with a red carnation in his buttonhole. He enjoyed golf and motoring and in 1945, after some success at the track, he bought a horse called Bernborough, which won fifteen races—after which he sold it to Hollywood mogul Louis B Mayer.

A New Year's Eve Gala Dinner menu from Romano's in 1952 gives some idea of the kind of food that Beppi would have served—and been confused by. The dinner began with *huîtres d'Hawkesbury River* and moved though to *velouté*

Carte du Jour

Above: Beppi at Bondi Beach in the early days in Sydney.

Roast and Grills

Minute Steak	4/6
Fillet Mignon Maitre d'Hotel	4/6
Royal Squab	7/6
Baby Double Lamb Chops Pommes Paille	4/6
Poulet de Grain Grilled Sauce Diable (Double Serve)	16/-
Lamb Cutlets	4/-

Vegetables

String Beans	1/-
Broccoli	1/6
Stewed Tomato	1/9
Asparagus	3/-
Peas	1/-
Brussels Sprouts	1/-
Carrots Vichy	2/-
Artichokes	1/-
Cauliflower	1/-
Whole Spinach	1/-

Potatoes

Fried	1/6
	1/6
...aise	1/9
Brown	1/9

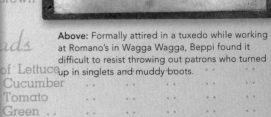

Above: Formally attired in a tuxedo while working at Romano's in Wagga Wagga, Beppi found it difficult to resist throwing out patrons who turned up in singlets and muddy boots.

Above: Beppi and his manager, Mr Gallo hosting a Christmas banquet night at the Romano Hotel in 1954.

Salads

...of Lettuce	1/-
...Cucumber	-/9
...Tomato	1/-
...Green	

Desserts

Pot de Creme	1/6
Cheese Cake	1/6
Meringue Glace	1/6
Zabaglione al Marsala	2/-
French Pastry	1/-
Mousse au Chocolate	

Romano's Restaurant

au lait d'amandes; *poussins à la Romano*; *asperges de Riverina en branche sauce citronette*; and *mince-pie maison*, followed by *café moka*. When shown this menu, Beppi added another dish from the time that he remembered well, *crêpes des fraises*, cooked tableside, with chopped strawberries and orange zest, the whole flamed in Strega liqueur and finished with a dollop of cream.

Azzalin Romano sold Romano's in 1964, and it was re-born as a discotheque with go-go girls. 'Azzalin the Dazzlin' as he was known, died in his harbour-side, Point Piper flat in 1972.

> Romano was very friendly with the Police Commissioner. He had a horse that won all the races. Naturally, Australians liked him because they love gambling. He used to get away with anything. He never minded the restrictions with licences and so on. He used to gamble with the top people. The police would never raid him. He used to refuse people at the door if they didn't look decent. I remember Percy Stewart Dawson, the man who brought Romano to Sydney. He was a skinny larrikin, pissed all the time. He had money, he did whatever he wanted.
>
> A fellow called Bonfante always cooked the steak Diane tableside and I watched him carefully. I think steak Diane was brought here by Azzalin Romano. It's cooked in a lot of butter. Before turning the steak, you add garlic, parsley, brandy and Worcestershire sauce. They used to reduce the sauce too much, and get too strong a flavour of Worcestershire. I didn't cook the meat in the brandy, I'd take the meat out, then do the brandy, add more butter and reduce the sauce and pan juices. When the sauce was nearly right, I'd put back the meat for a few minutes and add some chopped up parsley.

Just exactly who brought the curious dish, steak Diane, to Australia, and where it comes from is a hotly disputed issue. In 1996, the 'Short Black' column in the *Herald* 'Good Living' section published a series of responses from readers in pursuit of the origins of this quintessential 1950s dish. George Koolis, head waiter at the time at Chiswick Gardens restaurant in Woollahra maintained that the owner of that restaurant, Tony Geminis, invented it in London for 'the girlfriend of a royal personage', later identified as one Lady Diana Manners. Another correspondent, Edward Mansfield, contended that Geminis learnt the dish in London from Charles Gallo, who later came to Australia to manage Romano's in Wagga Wagga. Sydney chef Mark Armstrong weighed in with an excerpt from a book he had kept from his apprentice days entitled *Menu Terminology* (1969), which states that 'Diane … applies mainly to game or a game flavour, an exception being entrecôte'. The book asserts that the name comes from the goddess of hunters, or perhaps Diane de Poitiers (1499–1566) who 'exerted considerable influence over Henry II of France'. Margaret Fulton pinpointed The Ivy in London as the site of its invention, and two possible origins for its name: a French chef who named it for his daughter, or a Greek kitchen slang word for sauté pan. Just to throw a spanner into the sauté pan, another reader, Ed Webber, wrote with memories of learning to prepare the dish tableside in New York in the 1950s from ex-Cunard waiters, and finishing it by rolling the steaks—he called it 'crêpes for carnivores'. Other American sources for the dish include the Drake Hotel in New York (one Nino of the Drake claims to have introduced it there), The Colony restaurant also in New York, the Copacabana Palace Hotel in Rio de Janeiro, as well as restaurants in Belgium in the 1920s. Success, it appears, has many chefs.

After I'd been there a year, Romano's son, Renzo, took over as manager. He used to like me. He had an Italian girlfriend, she didn't want anybody else to cook anything for her but me. I was working in the bar at the time and there weren't many customers at lunch time, so she'd call me and I'd go out and cook steak Diane for her and Renzo. There was a bit of friction, you had all these waiters who spoke English well and dressed beautifully with the tails, and they didn't like me very much at all. When I used to cook they used to buzz around and keep checking what I was doing, so I'd put on a real show and flash the brandy flame.

I used to get £12 18s a week wages at Romano's, and about £9 a week in tips. After a year, somebody dobbed me in to the tax department. They asked me questions on how much I spent and how much I was banking. How could I be banking so much? I said, 'The tips'. They said, 'You have to pay tax on that'. I didn't know that. They could see it was an innocent mistake. They fined me and let me pay off the tax.

Exclusive Romano Features

Romano's Oyster Bar

Romano's has long been known for the quality of its Oysters and other Shell Fish, and here, in pleasant and somewhat unique surroundings, you may enjoy them served "just how you like them." Appropriate Wines and Ales are available to add to the appeal of these delicious Sea Foods.

Let our Chef suggest a Menu for you

Sometimes it is difficult to decide just what foods you would like. This is just the occasion when our Chef's suggestion could easily come as a happy solution of your problem. Ask your Waiter about it, and relax.

Individual Dishes

It is a happy thought, sometimes, to have individual dishes prepared at your own table for your guests. If you would like to do this, ask your Waiter to convey your wishes to the Manager, who will gladly see to it that they are carried out in a manner that will delight you.

Fresh Vegetables, Salads, Eggs and Poultry

The acknowledged excellence of Romano's Cuisine is due to a large extent to the fact that our own "Alicia" Farm furnishes continuous supplies of these products grown under ideal conditions.

Romano's Private Room for Parties

Romano's "Private Room" is charmingly appointed and is ideal for private parties up to thirty-five persons, and Romano's, in the best traditions of really fine catering, will see to it that insofar as choice Wines, delectable Foods and unrivalled Service are concerned, nothing will be left to chance to ensure a really delightful function for you.

Wines, Ales, Cigarettes and Cigars

The choicest Wines are usually available to you at Romano's, and it is suggested that you consult the Head Waiter regarding these. The finest brands of Cigars and Cigarettes, both Local and Imported, may be obtained also.

Romano's Specialities

Potted Shrimps
Lobster Flambe au Cognac
Prawns Newburg Riz Pilaff
Fillet of Sole Marie Therese

Fresh Noodles Napolitaine
Ravioli a la Mode Romano's
Spaghetti a la Marinara
Canneloni au Jus de Veau
Risotto Milanaise

Crepes des Volaille Princess Elizabeth
Rognons Saute Maison
Boeuf Strogonoff
Pilaff de Foie de Volaille Sauce Diable
Khebabb d'agneau Oriental
Supreme of Chicken Marina
Tournedo Saute Rossini
Supreme of Chicken aux Paprika
Escalopini of Veal Tony
Supreme de Volaille Kiewsky

Sabaillon au Sherry
La Crepe Romano
La Poire Mariette
Crepe Suzette
Mousse au Chocolate
Black Boy of Congo
Les Fraises Flambe au Cognac
(when in season)
La Coupe de Fruit Pompadour

When you may dine at Romano's

MONDAY TO SATURDAY

LUNCHEON	12 to 2.30
DINNER	6 to 9

With DANCING until 9.30

Reservations

Reservations may be made by Telephoning BW 4721.

For any discrepancies in the services or for any incivilities Patrons are kindly requested to contact the Management immediately.

To the bush. A date at the beach

In 1947, Azzalin Romano bought and rebuilt the Commercial Hotel in Wagga Wagga, re-naming it Romano's. History does not tell us the thinking behind this curious venture. The name, however, remains, and Romano's Hotel operates in Wagga (as it is known) to this day. It was the place to stay for the smart city/country set—an item in the *Herald* social pages for May 1952 noted that 'Miss Diane Field of Bellevue Hill joined her mother Mrs Jack Field at Romano's in Wagga'. Indeed, it was probably the only place to stay with any sort of amenities. Beppi was sent there to manage the dining room. It was not a good fit.

Situated on the Murrumbidgee River about 450 kilometres south-west of Sydney, Wagga takes its name from the word for 'crow' in the language of the original inhabitants, the Wiradjuri people (Wagga Wagga, a number of crows). It is today, and was in the 1950s, New South Wales' largest inland city. The region produces wheat, dairy, mixed farming and fat lambs—with the exception of wine grape growing today, much the same as it would have been in the 1950s.

It is fair to say that country towns in 1950s Australia, even large ones, were not known as centres of sophistication or gastronomic delights, especially compared to Venice, Florence and Rome. Indeed, it is recorded that the first Chiko Roll (a mass-produced food item modelled very loosely on the Chinese spring roll) was sold in Wagga Wagga in 1951. The population of Wagga Wagga in 1952 was approximately 20,000, predominantly farmers and farm workers and in the town itself, those working in their support industries.

> After two years at Romano's doing the lunch bar they sent me to Wagga Wagga. The director was Charles Gallo, and the chef and the second chef were both Italian. I was managing the dining room. Aldo Zuzza was a waiter there. We worked right through the summer, and we remained in our full waiter's dress with jackets and ties. Most of the patrons were guests at the hotel, they ate antipasto, pasta, scaloppini, roast chicken, roast lamb and steak Diane cooked by me at the table. They used to come in to the dining room in singlets and muddy boots and I tried to refuse them and they got upset.

Left: Romano's special features, including instructions to patrons should they encounter 'any incivilities'.

Mr Gallo came out and took me aside and said, 'These are the only kind of people we get here, so you've got to relax'. I left after a couple of months.

I didn't want to stay any longer. I was upset and confused. It was hard to adapt. When I came from Italy, I was a qualified chef de rang, and when you're a chef de rang in Italy, you're a qualified professional. I came over here, I got a job at Romano's in Sydney, quite a nice high-class place. Then they sent me to Wagga, and I tried to run the place the way I knew, but there were lots of impediments—for example the cashier, she kept trying to boss me around and tell me what to do. I had quite a few arguments with her. It wasn't a pleasant time.

Beppi returned to Sydney, and began working as a casual waiter at Prince's, Andre's, Chequers and also at Milano's in Elizabeth Bay (owned by Roy Milano), where Primo Fasetta was the chef and a partner. Beppi had a flat at Roslyn Gardens, which he shared with Aldo Zuzza, close to Milano's.

Roy Milano himself did the *guéridon* cooking at Milano's. Then in 1953, Roy Milano decided to open a restaurant at Edgecliff in partnership with (Beppi's future wife Norma Zaccaria's uncle) Bob Mazzaroli and another man—and he took the name Milano's with him. Primo Fasetti stayed in Elizabeth Bay and that became Primo's, with Primo cooking. 'I worked there with Natalino Proietti (who later had a restaurant in Kellett Street, Kings Cross called Natalino's).'

Later, I went to Milano's, doing the dinner service, and while I was there I got a licence as a taxi driver for during the day. I had to apply twice—the first time they rejected me because they said my English was not too good and I didn't know enough of the important places in Sydney. The first cab I drove broke down in the middle of the road in Edgecliff. They always gave the new drivers the worst cars in the fleet. And some passengers would abuse me and call me a wog, they'd try to get out of paying me.

During this period, Beppi went to New Zealand, working on the cruise ship *Wanganella* with Aldo Zuzza. It was meant to be a paid holiday and a chance to see a new country. During a storm he broke his wrist and was put ashore in Auckland to convalesce, then sent back to Sydney on another ship with full pay.

When I got back from New Zealand, I started driving a cab again, as well as working at Milano's. I was driving seven days a week and also working in the restaurant. I didn't get much sleep. I was driving one day, and I found myself on the footpath in Park Street in the city. I woke up and said to myself, you have to give up driving the taxi. At this time I was not happy. I was seriously thinking of going back home.

Then two things happened to change his mind. He found the site of what was to become Beppi's; and he met his future wife, Norma, at Milano's. Norma Zaccaria was Australian born, but her father Angelo came from Sandrigo in the province of Vicenze and her mother Teresa from Toppo in Udine. Both parents migrated before the war, and they met and married in Sydney in 1932. They had a furniture manufacturing business, Olympia Cabinet Company in Newtown, which they had leased out before Norma met Beppi. Beppi and Norma tell the story.

Norma: My Uncle Bob was one of the owners of the restaurant [Milano's]— he was my mother's brother. I was there for lunch. I'd just come back from a long trip to Italy with my parents. My father had leased his furniture business, and went into semi-retirement. I was there for lunch—and Beppi was working there.

Beppi: It was in the afternoon, I was coming back from a swim at Bondi. I was rushing because I was late.

Norma: I'd never seen him before and I said where've you been and he said I've been to the beach in Bondi and I said …

Beppi: Your uncle introduced me to you, then you asked me the question.

Norma: I said when are you going to take me to the beach. I was forward. He said he'd give me a ring, and when he did I said, oh I can't make it today and he said, now or not at all.

Beppi: I had an 1100 Fiat at the time and we used to go to the National Park on picnics—you remember?

Norma: Eventually we went to the beach.

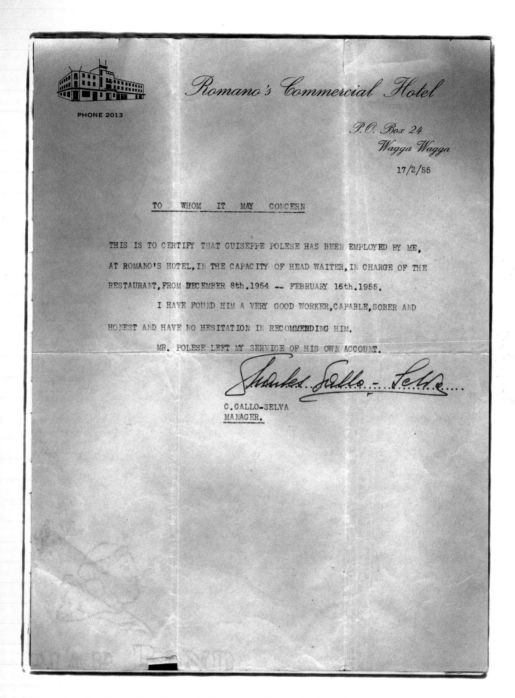

Romano's Commercial Hotel

PHONE 2013

P.O. Box 24
Wagga Wagga
17/2/55

TO WHOM IT MAY CONCERN

THIS IS TO CERTIFY THAT GUISEPPE POLESE HAS BEEN EMPLOYED BY ME,
AT ROMANO'S HOTEL, IN THE CAPACITY OF HEAD WAITER, IN CHARGE OF THE
RESTAURANT, FROM DECEMBER 8th.1954 — FEBRUARY 16th.1955.

I HAVE FOUND HIM A VERY GOOD WORKER, CAPABLE, SOBER AND
HONEST AND HAVE NO HESITATION IN RECOMMENDING HIM.

MR. POLESE LEFT MY SERVICE OF HIS OWN ACCOUNT.

C. GALLO-SELVA
MANAGER.

Above: Beppi's reference from Romano's, after a miserable couple of months in Wagga.

Continental cuisine

STEAK DIANE

You need to cook this dish using a gas cooktop. You can't flame it if you are using an electric one. Start with a piece of beef fillet for each person—about 200 g each and about 5-cm thick. Put it on a board and gently hammer it with a wooden or metal mallet (use a rolling pin if you don't have a mallet) so it spreads and becomes thin—less than 10-mm thick (these days you would put plastic wrap over the board before putting the meat on it and more on top).

Put a dob of butter in a frying pan and sizzle it until it is nice and hot. Pick up the meat with a fork, roll it around the prongs and then slowly unroll it into the sizzling butter, so it doesn't splash.

When one side is cooked—after about 1 minute—turn it and add a chopped-up garlic clove, parsley (with mixed-in celery leaves if you like), and 3 shakes of Worcestershire sauce to the pan. Add salt and pepper (but not too much because the Worcestershire sauce is already peppery).

Cook for a few seconds. Now here's the spectacular bit. Turn up the flame, pour in a generous slurp of brandy, tilt the pan so the brandy runs to the edge near the flame, and it will catch fire. Let it flare so the alcohol burns out, leaving the concentrated woody flavour.

When the flame is out, remove the meat and put it on a plate to one side. Add a bit more butter and reduce the sauce, simmering over a low heat for about 1 minute until it thickens. Too much heat will cause the butter to burn and separate. Pour the sauce over the meat. Serve with roast potatoes and spinach (on side plates so the sauces don't mix).

The spinach: Put butter and a little chopped garlic in a frying pan, then add chopped spinach. Add salt and pepper and cook on a low heat so the liquid released by the spinach comes off as steam. At Romano's they would add cream and butter and make a purée. I like to sprinkle parmesan cheese over it, because cheese and spinach is a lovely combination, which goes well with meat but is too strong for fish.

LOBSTER FOUR WAYS

At Romano's, the customers wanted elaborate lobster dishes because it was a way to show off their wealth. The recipe I knew from Italy was called 'all'Americana', but the Romano's favourites were thermidor, mornay and 'au cognac'. All of those methods seem strange to me now, because the heavy sauces drown the flavour of the seafood. These days I just serve lobster grilled with lemon, butter and parsley. But if you want to do some time travelling, here's how.

You need to start with raw lobster; use ones that have been freshly killed at the fishmonger. Never buy pre-cooked lobster meat, because reheating it will make it dry. Put the lobster flat on its stomach on a big board. Push the point of a big sharp knife through the lobster behind the head, with the blade pointing towards the head, and cut the head in half lengthwise. Then turn the knife around and cut the body in half. Open the halves out, take out the coral and the liver and set them aside. Throw away the guts (the bowel is in the lower part of the tail).

With a small sharp knife detach the meat from the shell at the back of the head without cutting it all the way along so it remains attached. Remove the head and legs. The tail contains the meat, while the head and legs can be used to make stock.

Crush the head and legs and simmer the bits in a pan with butter, onion, garlic, 2 chopped tomatoes, some celery and tarragon, salt and pepper, and splashing in some brandy. When the alcohol has evaporated, add 1 litre of water or fish stock and simmer for 1 hour. Strain out the solid ingredients, especially the bits of shell, and you have a stock.

Now you have your choice of methods ... (with these recipes, the meat is detatched from the shell and cut into pieces if required).

all' Americana: Fry the lobster's liver and coral in butter with chopped French shallots and the zests of a lemon and an orange. After 3 minutes add 1 cup of lobster stock, crushed garlic, 1 soupspoon of tomato paste, and sprinkles of cayenne pepper and saffron. Simmer. Cut the lobster tail into chunks about 2-cm wide (with the shell attached to the meat like a medallion) and put them into the sauce. Add a splash of brandy and a splash of Grand Marnier and simmer for 5 minutes. Take out the lobster pieces and put them on plates. Thicken the sauce with a little rice that has been overcooked in lobster stock and mashed, and pour the sauce over the lobster pieces.

Au cognac: Prepare the sauce as you would with all'Americana, up to the point that you throw in the lobster pieces. Simmer for 3 minutes then pour in a big splash of cognac, tilt the pan until the alcohol catches fire, and flame it in front of the guests. Simmer for another 3 minutes until the sauce is thick. Serve with rice or mashed potatoes.

Thermidor or Mornay: First make a béchamel, which means melting butter in a frying pan, stirring in flour, nutmeg, and slowly adding milk until it makes a smooth paste. To give a bit more flavour, you can add some fish stock, tarragon, cayenne pepper, 1 spoonful of tomato paste, and a little French mustard to the béchamel. No lemon, though.

Slice along the inside of the shell with your knife to loosen the meat, and then slice across the top of the meat to make chunks which are still partly attached to the shell so that the flavours can penetrate.

Splash a bit of brandy over the lobster (it goes well with shellfish). Spoon the béchamel over the lobster meat so it runs down and penetrates into the cuts you've made in the meat. That will mix with the juices of the lobster while you're cooking it. Then bake for about 5 minutes in an oven preheated to 180°C.

For lobster mornay, use the same béchamel, but don't include fish stock as you're making it. Add a little parmesan cheese to the sauce and pour it over the meat. After 5 minutes in the oven, take out the lobster halves and put a little slice of fontina (or another mild-flavoured cheese) over the béchamel. Then you can finish it under the griller so the cheese starts to brown, or put it back in the oven for 5 minutes. It looks interesting when served with rice, but to me, this is no way to treat a lobster. Cheese and fish just don't match.

BEEF STROGANOFF

Prepare your base: Heat a dob of butter in a frying pan and add onion and garlic. Cook until the onion has softened and become golden. Add a large handful of finely sliced mushrooms and fry them until most of the moisture has gone.

Cut a large beef fillet into thin strips (about 1 kg for four people). Lightly flour the strips. Toss the strips into the base (mushroom mixture), with ½ teaspoon of sugar, the juice of ½ lemon, a small splash of white vinegar and red wine vinegar, and a big splash of brandy. Simmer gently for 1 minute or so, then add 2 shakes of cayenne pepper, some finely chopped parsley and celery leaves, and ½ cup of cream. Stir and reduce for 1 minute. Serve with rice.

CHICKEN MARYLAND

This dish is too sweet for me, but in the '50s, a lot of people liked it. Use chicken breasts that still have the wing bone attached; this should be trimmed at the middle joint. At Romano's they put a little white paper cap on the end of the wing bone for decoration. Dip the chicken in flour, then in beaten egg, then crumb it (with salt, pepper and a little grated parmesan mixed with dried breadcrumbs). Fry in sizzling butter, but on not too high a heat or the breadcrumbs will burn without the centre of the chicken cooking.

Normally they served it with sliced pineapple that had also been crumbed and fried in butter. You put the pineapple on top of the chicken when you serve it. Some restaurants coated both the chicken and the pineapple (or even banana sometimes) in batter and and deep-fried them. This made the dish heavy as well as sweet. If you're going to try this, you should coat the pineapple in flour before you batter it, so it won't break up during cooking.

CHICKEN KIEV

Use the breast of the chicken with the fillet attached, about 150 g. Beat the breast out flat using a meat mallet between 2 pieces of plastic wrap. Toss it in flour. Beat

2 egg yolks with salt and pepper and chopped rosemary, and spread the mixture on the inside of the breast and fillet, with a dob of butter, and a little crushed garlic and some salt and pepper. Now roll the breast into a tight parcel so it looks like a fat banana. Dip the parcel in flour, then egg and roll it in a mixture of breadcrumbs and a little parmesan. The rolls should hold together but, if you want to be sure, you can secure them with toothpicks. Deep-fry for 5 minutes.

When you're serving the kiev, there's a risk the hot butter will spurt out when you puncture it, so put in the fork at the end away from your eyes. You can vary the filling with cheese, mushrooms or prosciutto if you prefer.

ZABAGLIONE

My mother used to give me zabaglione when I would come back home for the winter after working as a waiter through the season. She always said I was looking pale and tired, and the zabaglione would perk me up. So when I started working at Romano's and found most of the food so strange, I was comforted to find that zabaglione was one of their dessert specialities.

It's a dish you can make in front of the customer, who appreciates all your arm work. Use 2 egg yolks for each person served. Put them in a bowl with 1 soupspoon of sugar per person and whip them over a bigger bowl containing boiling water. Slowly pour in 1 sherry glass of marsala and ½ sherry glass of brandy and keep whipping; it is ready when it is fluffy and light. (My mother only used marsala, but the brandy gives a kick.) Serve it in a large warm glass.

Note: You can experiment with the alcohol you use for this dessert by replacing the brandy with rum.

CHAPTER FIVE

PERSUADING AUSTRALIANS TO TRY THE UNKNOWN

Left: Beppi making pasta for the food writer Ted Maloney in the 1960s.

THE TIMES
1956

SOVIET TROOPS AND TANKS CRUSHED AN UPRISING IN HUNGARY AND RECLAIMED BUDAPEST. MOROCCO GAINED ITS INDEPENDENCE FROM FRANCE AND SPAIN. ELVIS PRESLEY GYRATED HIS WAY TO FAME WITH HIS FIRST BIG HIT 'HEARTBREAK HOTEL'. GRACE METALIOUS' NOVEL *PEYTON PLACE*, ALWAYS DESCRIBED AS 'STEAMY', TOPPED THE BESTSELLER LISTS.

In Australia, the first televisions were switched on in September. The Olympics got underway in Melbourne in November. It was the beginning in Australian rock 'n' roll—Johnny O'Keefe's 'Wild One' was the hit of the year. In Sydney if they hadn't been working, Beppi and Norma could have sat at home and watched the film *Father Brown Detective*, or 'The Hucksters' on television.

The Sunday Herald, women's section offered a recipe for roast lamb with minted rice. 'It's Different!' the headline challenged. The reason for the recipe was to be found on the next page—an ad for Sunwhite Rice headlined 'With potatoes so scarce and costly, serve Sunwhite Rice'. No reason was given for the potato famine.

Also in the *SunHerald* that day was a story which featured a list of do's and don'ts for waiters based on a course that was starting at East Sydney Technical College by lecturer Len Barton. Some of Mr Barton's rules were:

Don't:
Encourage the woman to order for herself
Deal out plates like a poker hand
Shake a bottle of wine

Do:
Say hello and smile when people come to the table
Gain a knowledge of food and good wine
Show the wine to the host and allow him to test for bouquet,
colour and taste

According to Mr Barton, Australian waiters at the time were the second fastest in the world, 'but not the best'.

Getting started

On Sunday, 10 June 1956, a cold and showery day with blustering southerly winds, Beppi Polese and Norma Zaccaria went to the St James Café in Yurong Street, East Sydney, which Beppi—or rather the moneylender—now owned, and worked towards their opening the next day.

Norma didn't think much of the location: 'It was a terrible area, lots of street girls'. Norma was right. There had been a history of violence in the past, and in the 1920s it had been home to one Guido Caletti, a leading member of one of what were then known as 'razor gangs'. But curiously, and almost without knowing it, Beppi had chosen a location with many interesting and far more respectable Italian associations.

That part of Sydney from Yurong Street east to Palmer Street was Sydney's first Little Italy. Number 71–73 Stanley Street was home to the first known Italians in the area: Luciano and Maria Rizzi lived there from 1903 and set up a macaroni factory in 1911; and then in 1952, as already noted, it became La Veneziana—that name can still be seen, set in brass and terrazzo on the doorstep. In 1914, Vince Lopez, an Italian from the Aeolian Islands, opened a fruit shop at 82 Stanley Street, a business which, in the hands of another Lopez, Felice, lasted until his death in the 1950s. In 1928, George Famosa began a café, what is today The Arch Café and No Names Restaurant at 81 Stanley Street, and in 1933, Bartolomeo Callose established a pasta factory on the corner of Palmer and Burton Streets. But for Beppi, there was an even more personal reason for being here.

> When my father came to Australia in 1929, he lived in one of the boarding houses in the area, there were many of them, and the father of our friend Julie Elliott (she was born Julie Cinelli) owned two of them. Every time I see an old Italian man here I remember my father and I feel sad for him. He had left a wife and five children to come to a strange land to find work, and he

didn't succeed. One night, he left the boarding house, and someone stole the few pounds he had—which he had borrowed—from under his bed. Toni de Fort helped him then.

In her autobiography, *I Sang for My Supper* (1999), the doyenne of Australian food writers, Margaret Fulton, wrote 'by the mid-1950s, Australians were becoming more food conscious … With post war travel, the well-heeled were able to eat in restaurants like the Tour d'Argent in Paris … in London's Savoy or New York's Plaza …'

That may well have been so for the 'well-heeled' who, until not long after this period, were the only level of Sydney society to be found in the better restaurants. The not so well-heeled probably ate very much as one 2005 reviewer from *The Sydney Morning Herald* described The New York in Kellett Street in Kings Cross. Here chef John Kokaras had been cooking since 1955 with very little change in the menu—'a time before pasta, before confit, before Thai-style anything'—and this is what the reviewer ate:

> There's the steak with its white mashed potatoes, green peas, orange mashed pumpkin topped with a dollop of well-fried onion; chicken Maryland, ditto; four chump chops with a salad of torn iceberg, sliced beetroot and tomato. And two slices of brown bread with pats of butter.

Unless (like St James and La Veneziana over the road) restaurants were catering for what were then called 'New Australians', the food at The New York is the food most Australians were dining out on in the 1950s. Diners were there not to see or be seen, nor to be thrilled by exotic cuisine—even the 'local Chinese' was served from a small and well known repertoire of Australian–Chinese dishes—but, like the diners at The New York in 2005, because they were away from home or had no one at home to cook for or with.

It was, in retrospect, a very good year for a determined and talented Italian professional to open a restaurant in Sydney. Australians were ready for a food revolution—they'd had enough of chump chops and steak and chicken Maryland, even if they were well cooked—and Beppi Polese was in the front line of that revolution which was not just culinary, but social.

When I got here, I never thought to open a restaurant, just to work and earn enough money. Then I saw an advertisement saying this café was for sale. It was called St James, and it was owned by some Yugoslav people. They wanted £4500 for it—a lot of money then—I had no money of my own, only an 1100 Fiat and a few hundred pounds.

I was supposed to go into business with Aldo Zuzza. He decided against the deal, but he lent me £1000 and I borrowed £3500 from a moneylender.

Today, if you go into business you already know what's happening, how much you spend, and you have a plan. Then, I had no idea. I was just hoping to make enough to cover my instalments on the loan. I was prepared to work hard to survive.

I retained the staff, and served the same food, things like dumplings and schnitzel, chicken soup, goulash and toasted sandwiches. People would come in and pay for six meals by coupon in advance—4s 6d for a week of entrée, main course and a sweet. We didn't have a liquor licence, but we'd serve wine in a teacup and include it in the price of the meal. I continued with the Yugoslav menu for three years, working to pay back the loan.

At that time, the licensing laws in Sydney for restaurants and hotels were ludicrous. Wine had to be ordered before a certain time—it varied, sometimes 6 pm, sometimes 9 pm—or a bottle had to have the name of the customer written on it to preserve the fiction you had ordered it before you came. Only the year before (February, 1955) had the law changed to allow hotels to open after 6 pm (until 10 pm) ending the notorious 'six o'clock swill'. Beppi's was granted a licence in 1959.

We had very little money after paying the monthly on the loan, so we had to be smart. We did a deal with the refrigeration people—they gave us a new fridge and we paid with meals. A man called Laurie White used to do our printing for us and we also paid him with meals. It was barter. At first, we opened for lunch and dinner, seven days a week. Our first customers were working class people, they always had an early dinner. At 10 o'clock the place was empty.

At first Norma only worked at the restaurant after she finished her job in the office at O'Brien's (an electrical contractor)—she'd come in at five, often

Below: Beppi in the first year of the restaurant, when he startetd to gradually introduce diners to recipes from his homeland.

Above: Beppi's became a magnet for people interested in Australia's newly emerging food culture; here Beppi is serving cookery writer, Margaret Fulton.

Below: Paying off the restaurant loan was Beppi's primary concern in the early years, and he meticulously recorded his weekly earnings as he inched towards becoming debt-free.

Above: It took some years for Beppi to transform his restaurant into an impeccable fine dining experience for his patrons, and for diners to transform themselves into his sophisticated clientele.

with our friends John and Julie Elliott, and help collect the meal tickets. After two years, Norma came in full time. And gradually I changed the menu.

I remember at that time the chef at Milano's would buy chickens and only use the breast—they used to give me the legs for nothing—so I stuffed the leg with ham and cheese, and also we'd chop them up and make stuffed cabbage roll and stuffed capsicum, which I remembered from the roof garden at the Baglioni in Florence.

We'd also de-bone the thigh, flatten the meat, roll it, stuff it with cheese and make a chicken involtini with ham (we still have involtini on the menu). Then slowly I introduced pasta onto the menu—the first was ragù bolognese—there was also eggplant parmigiana, cannelloni and chicken liver pâté.

Back then it was difficult for Beppi to even find the ingredients he needed. But find them he did. In 1956, the wholesale fruit, vegetable and fish markets were still in the Haymarket, where they had been located off and on since 1869. Scattered among the fruit and veg and fish stalls were importers, delicatessens and smallgoods butchers—among them Fiorelli, Scala Brothers, Panuccio, Gavagna and one delicatessen still trading in the area, Cyril's, a true 'Continental' deli, with its original owner, Cyril Vincenc, still on the premises. Cyril's is the Beppi's of delis, having opened in the same year.

Beppi's restaurant was much smaller then than it is today. The kitchen was to the right of the front door, and the main—and only—dining room was to the left, which is the front room today. When they moved in, the room was painted a high-gloss pink, which Norma especially hated. They redecorated quickly. Arches were built, the ceiling was beamed, and the walls were painted to look like wooden lining up to the picture rail. The walls above the railing were painted light brown. There were ten tables, seating about forty people.

Later, carriage lamps that Beppi made himself were hung, and the art teacher Professor Bissietta (he taught at his own school, the Dattilo-Rubbo School), painted the first of two frescos at Beppi's, a fishing boat, in an alcove at the back of the dining room. Rush-bottomed chairs supplied by Norma's father's old business, Olympia, added to the rustic feeling of the room. The chairs are there to this day, the rush covered by padded leather cushions.

We used to buy our pasta from Gavagna and Fiorelli, who would make their pasta by hand just like my mother used to do—they were on one side of the markets selling groceries and on the other was the fish market. I'd go to the markets every day to buy salami, pasta and olive oil. Norma's family would help me quite a lot too, and I'd get herbs and spices and some vegetables from their friends. I didn't buy much fish because by that time I'd met two Italian fishermen, brothers Joe and Frank Crisafi, and they'd bring the catch of the day to the restaurant.

Crisafi used to bring me squid, octopus and sardines. I asked him about mussels. 'Oh yes', he said, 'there are quite a lot around the Spit Bridge'. So I bought a rubber dinghy from him, and Norma and I would go and collect the mussels, first from the Spit Bridge, and then, when they pulled it down to build a new one, from under the pier at Luna Park.

You have to pick the mussels on the low tide because when the tide is high, the surface of the water is always a bit dirty, and the mussels absorb this. But when it's low, all the dirt has floated out. So no matter what time the low tide was—it could be two in the morning—Norma and I would go and collect the mussels. We were tired, we'd been working all day. Then Crisafi said, 'I can get you the mussels from an Italian fisherman down south', so he brought them in too.

I would take them back to the restaurant and cook them simply as *cozze alla marinara* in a fish stock made from fish bones and heads I bought from Nick Ruello at the fish market in the Haymarket. I'd put them on the table, the same with the calamari, which I'd cook *in umido* (stewed in a small amount of liquid) and ask people to try them. They had to acquire the taste.

I had a special way of doing this. At first when they asked me what it was they were being offered and I told them, they'd say, 'Oh, I don't want that'. So because I had that experience of being rejected, next time I was asked 'What is it?', I'd say, 'You try it, then I tell you'. I remember using this trick much later with Lady (Mary) Fairfax (the wife of Sir Warwick, then the owner of John Fairfax & Sons, publishers of the *Herald*). She tried it and she said it was beautiful. I learnt they rejected everything—calamari, mussels, even baby sardines. But I had to make it work. I had Mr Smith (the moneylender) on my back.

And acquire the taste and talk they did. Before long, the word spread. Czechoslovakian-born art dealer, wine judge and member of the Wine and Food Society, Rudy Komon—who had also come to Australia in 1952—found the restaurant, ate, and returned with other members including Sydney advertising man and bon vivant, Snow Swift, and winemaker/surgeon Max Lake. Neville Baker, who was Foodmaster of the society from 1960 to 1970, described the food at Beppi's as 'brilliant'. In *Wogfood* (1996), a book about migrant influence on Australian food culture, Max Lake said, 'Beppi's was the sun coming over the horizon, because although we knew Australian–Greek food and Australian–Chinese food, the first taste of really authentic Italian food we had in Sydney was at Beppi's'.

Australian–Chinese (as opposed to real Chinese) food has been a feature of the country since the gold rush days in the 1850s, when one John Alloo set up a restaurant in the diggings at Ballarat, Victoria soon after they began. In Sydney's Dixon Street—the heart of Chinatown—'cookhouses' serving rudimentary meals for market workers and adventurous Australians before World War Two were replaced by restaurants—the first of which was probably the long-closed Lean Sun Low, which opened its doors in the late 1940s, quickly followed by others. Back then, all served similar dishes: sweet and sour pork, beef in black bean sauce, fried rice and lemon chicken. Such restaurants were in every country town and also swept through the suburbs.

Many of the Greeks who came to Australia ended up running milk bars (the Australian equivalent of American drug stores) or restaurants in country towns. They quickly adapted and rather than trying to get Australians to eat Greek food, they learnt how to cook steak and eggs, chops and eggs, and boiled chicken salads. Only the names of their restaurants and milk bars gave away their nationality: the Parthenon, the Acropole and the Paragon among them. In Sydney, the Hellenic Club in Elizabeth Street was where local Greeks went to eat and socialise. When Sydney restaurateur Dimitri Karageorge arrived in 1950, he quickly found the club and ate at the upstairs restaurant. Later, non-Greek Australians discovered it (it's still operating) and the New Hellas down the road, and began to enjoy souvlaki, moussaka and slow-roasted lamb.

Other regulars at Beppi's in those early days were members of the Fiorelli, Cantarella and Gavagna families and Sir James Hardy of the South Australian winemaking family.

The wedding, the chef and the wine cellar

On 9 November 1959, Beppi and Norma were married by a Capuchin monk at St Fiacre's in the inner-western suburb of Leichhardt, where Norma's parents attended Mass from time to time. Aldo Zuzza was Beppi's best man. Beppi's own parents remained in Italy—the cost of the journey beyond their grasp. The reception was at Milano's in Edgecliff, which Norma remembers as 'a big house with a garden on the side—it was a very lovely restaurant'. The food was prepared by the chefs at Milano. It was a joyous day for all concerned.

And then in 1960, the first stage of the total transformation of Beppi's walked in the door. A Neapolitan chef, Giuseppe Arena.

> The Wine and Food Society people would come every Friday and say to me, 'Cook what you want'. They'd bring a bottle of wine wrapped up in newspaper and then try and guess what it was. There were about fourteen of them. We used to cook guinea fowl and pheasant from a farm owned by friends of my parents-in-law. There were also painters who came with Rudy Komon, like William Dobell and Sidney Nolan. They used to bring paintings and show them and argue about prices with buyers who Rudy Komon would bring to lunch.
>
> At the time I wasn't interested in painting—I was interested in money to pay my debts—stupid! Once Russell Drysdale drew a cheque for £150 on a napkin—I said I'm sorry I can't accept that, I need cash to pay off my loan. If only I had known, I could have sold that cheque. Somebody else at the lunch that day said, 'I'll pay the bill, and I'll take the napkin'. [In spite of having his hand-drawn cheque rejected by Beppi, Russell Drysdale drew two beautiful little sketches in the visitor's book.]

Beppi had begun his interest in Australian wines very early, from the time of getting a licence in 1959. But now, he was beginning to build a serious cellar, with some fine Australian and European wines.

Right: It was with mixed emotions that Beppi celebrated his marriage—while he was thrilled to be marrying Norma, he was sad that his family weren't there to share his happiness.

Even before I got a licence, Rudy Komon used to sell me Saltram wines, riesling and shiraz—no labels—I learnt from them, they were very different from Italian wines. It was the start of the success of the Australian wine industry, slowly they learnt and improved.

I was very friendly with Mr Gower, the man from Seppelt's. Every time they released a vintage wine, I was the first one to choose. One day he came with a bottle and he said, 'Look, I've just come from wine testing and I've got this bloody plonk here, let's taste it'. It was the first [Penfold] Grange [Hermitage]. In the beginning, Grange is harsh and tannic, it's good after fifteen or more years. Back then it did taste like plonk. Back then they didn't know what would happen to it with age. I recently opened a bottle of the 1956 at Tetsuya's [another celebrated Sydney restaurant] with Norma and Marc [his son]. It was beautiful. But I bought a couple of bottles back then. I could have had a lot more for very little. Today I've got all the vintages [of the Grange] from 1954 [it was first produced in 1951] to the recent vintage, except about four.

There was a member of the Wine and Food Society who had bought some wine to the restaurant, and I remember them talking about it. This fellow said, 'It's no bloody good'. Rudy Komon was there and he knew this wine. He said, 'I'll buy it from you' and the fellow gave it away for practically nothing. A while later Rudy Komon brought a bottle of wine and they had a tasting—wrapping the bottles in newspaper to hide the labels. And the fellow who had given the wine away said, 'This is a magnificent wine, Rudy, what is it?' Rudy said, 'I can sell you some, I've got a couple of dozen'. And he sold him the wine he'd given away.

I faded the Yugoslavian food out when Giuseppe Arena came to work for me in 1960. We started doing Neapolitan type food—cannelloni and lasagne—and by 1963 we appeared as a proper Italian restaurant. We were very busy, with a queue on the footpath. There were only three or four of us working, Norma was at the counter, we'd take the orders to the kitchen without dockets, just by word of mouth.

At the time, we put in an exhaust fan in the kitchen to take out the odours. One morning, I was rushing in the front door carrying a wooden crate full of lettuces, when a man stopped me. 'What's the smell?', he asked.

I said, 'It's the smell from the kitchen'. He said, 'People are complaining about the smell—what kind of food are you cooking?' I said, 'Italian'. 'Oh', he said, 'Wog food'. I dropped the crate of lettuce and shook his hand. '*Grazie*', I said, '*grazie!*' I thought it was a compliment. I think I dropped the crate on his foot.

But not everyone complained. One day a couple came in. They said, 'We were going to Repin's [a café in the city] but we followed the wonderful smell and we came here'. After that I told the chef to put on a pot of garlic, onion and tomato every morning—and to put it under the exhaust fan so the smell would go out onto the street. It was a fantastic time, we were serving real Italian food.

All the money we made at that time, we put back in the business. By 1961, I had paid it all back.

Around this time Beppi's was beginning to get mentions in the social pages, quite possibly the first sure sign of success in Sydney at the time: 'Wednesday, June Hordern gave a dinner at Beppi's with Mari Livingston and David Vincent', read a notice in *The Daily Telegraph* in 1962.

But the best was yet to come—for Beppi and Norma—the birth of their son Marc in 1961, and then an award that would transform the restaurant.

Real Italian

STUFFED CAPSICUMS

This is one of the earliest dishes we served at Beppi's. I like yellow or red capsicums, but any colour will do. Slice around the stalk to remove the top, then take out the core and the seeds. Keep the top. Now make the stuffing. In a big pot, fry 1 onion in olive oil for about 5 minutes, add a handful of minced chicken meat and veal (or you could use chopped-up ham or Italian sausage) and fry for another 3 minutes. Add some rice, enough to fill the capsicum when it is cooked, and cook for a few minutes to absorb the cooking juices.

Now slowly add about ½ litre of chicken stock (or less and make it up with a little wine) and some salt and pepper. It's a kind of risotto (see chapter 2) but it doesn't need as much stirring. Cook for about 10 minutes, until the stock is absorbed. Remove from the heat, let the rice cool and then stir through 1 beaten egg, a handful of diced mozzarella cheese, a minced clove of garlic, and 1 large spoon of chopped parsley. Now spoon this mixture into the capsicums until they are full. Replace the tops of the capsicums and put them in a baking dish with a little olive oil in the bottom and splash some more oil over them. Put 1 spoon of chopped raw tomato and basil on top of each capsicum. Bake in the bottom part of a 160°C oven for 20 minutes and serve.

SPAGHETTI BOLOGNESE

This is another early dish from the restaurant and one of the most popular Italian dishes around, which I knew as ragú. Use 1 kg of beef or a mixture of ½ kg pork and ½ kg beef. It can be cheap meat because the cooking makes it tender. Coarsely mince the meat (or get your butcher to mince it for you) and brown it in a pan, throwing away the watery juice that comes out of the meat. In a separate saucepan, fry 4 onions, 3 cloves of garlic, 4 sticks of celery (the small ones from the heart of the bunch), 4 small carrots, some rosemary, pepper and bay leaves in a mixture of butter and oil for 5 minutes, then add the meat. Splash in ½ litre of white wine and simmer until the alcohol evaporates. Now throw in 6 chopped tomatoes—don't remove the skin because the flavour is there—and 1 teacup of tomato paste. Simmer for 10 minutes, then add 1 litre of chicken stock. Simmer for 2 hours or more. Add ground pepper and salt to taste. It gets better if kept overnight.

The spaghetti: I always believe pasta should be partly cooked in its sauce. Pasta is a greedy element, so it will absorb the flavour of the sauce. Boil the spaghetti in salted water for about 5–7 minutes, drain it and simmer it in the Bolognese sauce for another 5 minutes or longer. Serve with lots of grated parmesan.

MUSSELS

Use only fresh mussels—allow about 500 g per person. They should be closed. Scrub the outsides, and pull off their beards. Put ½ cup of fish stock in the bottom of a pot with some olive oil, parsley and 1 chopped garlic clove. Heat the mixture and then throw in the mussels with 1 finely chopped tomato and ½ cup of white wine. Put the lid on the pot, turn up the heat and within 2 minutes they should have opened and put out their own tasty water. (Throw away any that haven't opened.) Serve with crunchy bread for dipping in the liquid.

Alternatively, you can do stuffed mussels. Steam them in the pot for 1 minute with just a little fish stock and olive oil at the bottom. As soon as they have opened, take them out of the liquid, remove the top shells and cover each mussel with a paste made by mixing dried breadcrumbs, minced garlic, parsley, butter, salt, pepper, anchovies and a little of the liquid they were cooked in. Put them in a baking dish with more of the liquid from the bottom of the original cooking pot and bake in a 160°C oven for 5 minutes.

SQUID

The simplest way to introduce people to calamari is in the form of a salad. To serve four people, you need about 500 g of squid(s). Clean the squid (cut out the eyes and beak and carefully remove the ink sac and the internal bone that looks like a piece of plastic), then wash under cold water. Now put them in 1 litre of cold water with ¼ cup of white wine vinegar and 1 teaspoon of salt, some bay leaves, 1 cut onion and a little chilli, then cover and simmer for half an hour. Turn the heat off and leave them to cool in the pot. Drain them, and then cut them into strips. Sprinkle the squid with olive oil, lemon juice, crushed garlic and some chopped parsley and celery leaves. Serve with quartered lemons.

More interesting is squid stuffed with their own legs. For this you need bigger squid—one per person. Clean them, and set the ink sacs aside for use later. Cut the tentacles off the head and finely chop them. Mix the tentacles with finely chopped garlic, onion, parsley, breadcrumbs, salt, pepper, 2 eggs to bind, and a little butter. Fill the bodies with this mixture, and secure them with a toothpick so the stuffing cannot escape. Now sauté the bodies in a saucepan with oil for 2 minutes, splash in ½ cup of wine and squeeze the ink from the ink sacs over them. Cover the pan and simmer on low heat for 20 minutes, adding a little tomato and tomato paste. Serve with boiled rice or grilled polenta (see chapter 1).

CUTTLEFISH

Once people are familiar with calamari, they should have no trouble with *seppie* (cuttlefish), which makes a lovely stew with peas. Clean 500 g of cuttlefish per person (remove the bone for your budgie, throw away the beak and the insides, and keep only the hood and the legs for cooking). Slice the hood into strips. Brown 2 chopped onions for 5 minutes in a frying pan with some olive oil, then add rosemary and the sliced cuttlefish. Cook, stirring, for about 10 minutes, then add chopped parsley mixed with celery leaves, 3 crushed anchovies, 1 soupspoon of tomato paste and 4 chopped tomatoes (or a tin of tomatoes). Add ½ glass of white wine and ½ glass of water or fish stock. Simmer for 30 minutes until the sauce is reduced and the cuttlefish is tender. Add 100 g of fresh peas and cook for 5 more minutes. Serve with mashed potatoes or polenta.

ARTICHOKES

Try to buy fresh young artichokes. They should be a burgundy colour, long rather than round and not too big, so they won't yet have developed a beard inside.

Remove the outer leaves and the leaves around the base of the flower, then cut the tips off the remaining leaves so the top is flat and even. Trim the end off the stalk and peel the outer fibrous layer off it. Store the artichoke in water with the juice of ½ lemon, so the stalk doesn't go dark.

Put all the bits you have cut off the artichoke in 1 litre of water and boil for at least 1 hour to make a stock. This gives a concentrated flavour that is bitter by itself but useful to enhance the final result.

Now, hold the stalk and bang the flower on a board so the leaves open up and create space for the stuffing—which is a mixture of chopped garlic, breadcrumbs, parmesan, chopped mint, celery leaves, salt, pepper and a dob of butter to hold it together. Stuff this into the leaves.

Cut the stalk off each artichoke. Put a little oil and butter in a saucepan and sit the artichokes upright in a saucepan with the stalks between them. Splash olive oil over them and simmer on a low heat for 5 minutes with a lid on the pot.

Splash white wine on each artichoke and cook for another 5 minutes. Now pour in the artichoke stock so it reaches just below the top of the artichoke flowers. Now cook gently for 1 hour, or until tender.

Serve 2 artichokes and their stalks per person, with a little of the sauce from the pot poured over them. Explain to your guests that they don't have to eat all the leaves. They can chew on the outer leaves to suck the delicious juice out, and only eat the inner leaves, the base and the stalk. Provide plenty of toasted bread for soaking up the juice.

Young artichokes are also delicious fried. Pull off the outer leaves and cut off the tops of the remaining leaves with scissors. Cut off the bottom of the stalk. Soak the artichokes for 1 hour in water and lemon.

Slice the artichokes into quarters lengthways, dry them, toss them in flour and dip them in beaten eggs, then breadcrumbs. Heat some oil in a frying pan and fry the artichoke quarters for about 6 minutes on each side until golden. Take them out and place them on a paper towel to soak off any excess oil. Sprinkle with salt and pepper, and serve with lemon wedges.

Note: If you can only find older artichokes, pull off most of the leaves, then cut across the artichoke to separate the remaining leaves from the base and stalk. Scoop out the beard. Use the leaves only for stock. Cook the stalk and base in a frying pan with butter, oil, garlic and parsley, and after 5 minutes sprinkle with wine, stock, salt and pepper. Cook for 15 minutes on a low heat until the sauce has reduced, then serve.

Above: Beppi's parents, Caterina and Antonio, who were unable to come to Australia for their youngest child's wedding.

Below: Beppi and Norma on their wedding day.

Below: Marc's christening in 1961, clockwise from bottom left, friends John and Julie Elliott, Norma's grandmother, Norma's parents Angelo and Teresa Zaccaria, baby Marc, Norma, friends Norma and Natalino Proietti, and Beppi.

Below: Beppi and Marc in 1962.

Right: Beppi's takings book from May, 1963.

Below: Beppi with his Neopolitan chef, Giuseppe Arena. Once Giuseppe came on board, Beppi's completed the transition to serving a completely Italian cuisine.

Above: Marc and friend during a brief trip to Italy in the mid-1960s.

Beppi's

APPETISERS

	Entree
TOMATO or PINEAPPLE JUICE	30c
GREEN or BLACK ITALIAN OLIVES	40c
SALAME ITALIANO	50c
PATE MAISON (home made)	80c
PRAWN COCKTAIL (cocktail sauce)	80c
ANTIPASTO MISTO (hors d'oeuvres varies)	90c
PROSCIUTTO é MELONE (Italian smoked ham, served with rock melon)	90c

OYSTERS

	Doz.	½ Doz.
OYSTERS NATURAL (cocktail sauce)	1.40	80
FRIED OYSTERS (egged, crumbed and fried)	1.60	1.00

MUSSELS

	Entree
MUSSELS alla MARINARA	$1.10

SOUPS

MINESTRONE (Italian vegetable soup)	50c
RISO in BRODO (clear rice soup)	50c
STRACCIATELLA ROMANA (clear soup, with egg yolks beaten up with grated cheese)	60

FARINACEOUS

	Entree	Dinner
CANELLONI (rolled pasta filled with minced chicken and meat, baked with grated cheese)	90c	1.50
LASAGNE VERDI al FORNO (baked green pasta)	90c	1.50
SPAGHETTI alla CARBONARA (ham, cheese and egg sauce)	70c	1.50
SPAGHETTI MARINARA (sea food sauce)	90c	1.50
RAVIOLI PIEMONTESE (bolognaise sauce)	80c	1.40
SPAGHETTI BOLOGNESE (meat sauce)	70c	1.30
SPAGHETTI alla GENOVESE (fresh basil sauce)	80c	1.40

FISH

FRITTO MISTO (mixed fried fish, tartare sauce)	1.90
FILLET of JOHN DORY LIVORNAISE (fresh tomato and white wine sauce)	2.00
CALAMARI FRITTI (fried fillets of squid, tartare sauce)	1.90
FILLET of JOHN DORY MEUNIERE (butter and lemon sauce)	2.00

MIXED DISHES

ESCALOPPE of VEAL al CARCIOFO (slices of veal, cooked with heart of artichokes)	2.0
VEAL al PROSCIUTTO (chopped ham and fresh cream sauce)	2.0
SCALOPPINE alla PARMIGIANA (veal crumbed in parmesan cheese)	1.9
VEAL au BEURRE (veal cooked with butter and parsley sauce)	1.9
FRIED CRUMBED LAMB'S BRAINS (egged, crumbed and fried)	1.9
SCALOPPINE al MARSALA (veal cooked with marsala wine)	1.9
CHICKEN LIVERS al ROSMARINO (rosemary flavouring)	2.0
VEAL ESCALOPPE CACCIATORA (sauted with mushrooms and red wine)	2.0
LOIN of PORK SICILIANA (sauce of capers, tomato and white wine)	2.0
VEAL SORENTINA (slices of veal with an egg plant sauce)	2.0
OSSO BUCO MILANESE (veal shank cooked with a white wine and mushroom sauce, served with rice)	2.0

MINIMUM CHAR

RESTAURANT

WINNER OF THE
1963
GOLDEN FORK
AWARD

STEAKS

SIRLOIN STEAK BOLOGNESE (topped with ham, cheese and grilled)	2.10
GRILLED SIRLOIN STEAK (sirloin grilled, with chef's garnish)	1.80
SIRLOIN STEAK al BARDOLINO (wine and garlic sauce)	2.00
SIRLOIN STEAK PIZZAIOLA (capers, capsicum and fresh tomato sauce)	2.00
STEAK DIANE (served with side salad)	2.20
GRILLED FILLET STEAK	2.00
FILET MIGNON	2.20
(Mushrooms ~~1/6~~ 60c extra)	

POULTRY

LEG of CHICKEN PAESANA (cooked with wine and fresh tomato)	1.80
CHICKEN LEG CACCIATORA (sauted with mushrooms and red wine)	1.80
CHICKEN LEG in CASEROLA (mushroom and mixed vegetable sauce)	1.90
BREAST of CHICKEN BOLOGNESE (topped with ham and melted cheese)	2.10
BREAST of CHICKEN CACCIATORA (sauted with mushrooms and red wine)	2.10
FRIED BREAST of CHICKEN (cooked to a golden brown)	2.00
GRILLED HALF CHICKEN—to order 20 minutes	2.10

CHEESE

IMPORTED BEL PAESE	(served with crisp biscuits)	60c
CAMEMBERT CHEESE	„ „ „ „	60c
IMPORTED DANISH BLUE	„ „ „ „	60c
NEW ZEALAND EPICURE	„ „ „ „	60c

SIDE SALADS

MIXED ITALIAN SALAD	(tossed in oil and vinegar)	30c
SLICED TOMATO SALAD	„ „ „ „ „	30c

SWEETS

LEMON GELATO	60c
CASSATA SICILIANA (home made)	70c
ZABAGLIONE al MARSALA (served with Italian savoiardi biscuit)	80c
CHOCOLATE CAKE (topped with whipped cream)	60c
ICE CREAM (caramel or chocolate sauce)	60c
FRESH STRAWBERRIES (cream or ice cream)—in season	80c
CREMA CARAMEL (cream caramel)—topped with cream	70c
FRUTTA ASSORTITA (fresh fruit from the basket)	
CAFFE NAPOLETANA (filtered coffee)	20c
(fresh cream)	10c

ner Only 2.00)

VINTAGE 1979
SPECIAL VINTAGE
Penfolds
ST. HENRI
CLARET
Bottled by
PENFOLDS WINES PTY. LTD.
MAGILL
STH. AUSTRALIA
750 ml

CHAPTER SIX

FAME WITH THE GOLDEN FORK AWARD

THE TIMES
1963

POPE JOHN XXIII DIED IN 1963. IN ENGLAND JOHN PROFUMO RESIGNED OVER THE CHRISTINE KEELER AFFAIR. MARTIN LUTHER KING DELIVERED HIS 'I HAVE A DREAM' SPEECH IN AUGUST. IN NOVEMBER, PRESIDENT JOHN F KENNEDY WAS ASSASSINATED.

In Australia, the attention of the nation was on the royal visit. On Tuesday, 12 March, *The Sydney Morning Herald* published photographs of a 'happy and relaxed' Queen Elizabeth and Prince Phillip gazing at the foreshores of the proposed Canberra lakes project.

By 1963, the ladies who lunched in the women's pages of the *Herald* had replaced their big hats with big hair. On 12 June—a day when the team at Beppi's were preparing the meal for the judges of the Golden Fork Award dinner—Mrs Bill Ryan and Mrs Ben Hanson displayed the efforts of their hairdressers while lunching at the Chevron Hilton Hotel after a charity fashion parade.

Italian fashion had taken the men of Sydney by the feet: shoemaker Julius Marlow advertised a dangerously pointed black dress shoe—'Veneto'—billed as 'top fashion in the Italian tradition' for £5 9s 11d. Pier Paolo Pasolini's controversial neo-realist film *Accatone* opened in Sydney amid some apprehension.

The *Herald* offered recipes for lobster in cheese sauce and 'gay' pineapple cakes. The word gay was then used in its original sense—elsewhere in the paper an advertisement urged readers to visit gay Adelaide.

In *The Daily Mirror*, restaurant reviews of a sort had begun to appear. Two pages entitled 'Goings on about town', edited by the pseudonymous Elizabeth Pitt, offered potted reviews under such headings as 'Mostly for Food' and 'Wine and Dine'. The food at Milano's (now under new ownership) was described as 'Continental cookery' and at The Lantern in Paddington as 'cosmopolitan cookery.'

Left: Beppi and Giuseppe Arena with the Golden Fork Award.

From goulash to ragù Bolognese

In 1962, Beppi and Norma were living in an apartment above the restaurant in the St James building, which Beppi had started renting the year before they were married. Also in 1962, Beppi's mother, Caterina, came out for a visit. Soon after, the Polese's bought a small house in Double Bay, then a larger one nearby which they demolished and re-built.

> In 1962, Aldo Zuzza sponsored his younger brother Giuseppe (Beppino) to come to Australia. I said to my mother, 'Why don't you come with him?' She wouldn't have been able to come on her own, but she came out with Beppino, and stayed with us first in the apartment above the restaurant, and later in our first house in Double Bay. She used to baby-sit Marc—both the grandmothers wanted to baby-sit him. She stayed for about nine months and then she said she wanted to go home. She said, 'Look, I feel happier in San Giovanni among people who speak my dialect'. I said, 'Mamma, you're here, we're happy to have you here, but you must do what you want'. She wanted to go home.

By then, Aldo Zuzza was working at Beppi's—he had begun in 1958 and managed the restaurant while Beppi and Norma honeymooned on the Gold Coast. And in 1961, after selling Milano's in Edgecliff, Bob Mazzaroli joined the team on the floor, which also included Victor Alexander. 'We were a good team working together then', remembers Beppi. 'Very professional.'

Beppi advertised for a second chef in 1963 and Marino Gullo, a young chef from the Aeolian Islands, joined Arena in the kitchen. Things were hotting up down on Yurong Street. The 'dream team' was in place. And then Alitalia flew in the front door.

> We started to be very busy. I think it was the variety of dishes—nobody was offering such variety in Sydney, certainly not in an Italian restaurant.

The word was getting out.

And then in 1963 Commendatore Beghe, the president of the Italian Chamber of Commerce told me that the chamber was helping to organise a competition—the Golden Fork Awards—among the Italian restaurants in Sydney as a promotion for Alitalia, who were going to start flying to Sydney from Rome the following year. And he asked, 'Would you like to compete?' And we said, 'Of course'.

I can't remember all the restaurants in the competition—there were six— but I remember two of them were Chianti [then in Elizabeth Street in the city] and Grotto Capri [still operating under different management on Anzac Parade in Kensington]. We had to produce a four-course menu and the wine to go with the food. And of course the menu had to balanced without any repetition of ingredients.

For 1963 Sydney, the menu was astonishingly sophisticated, and only a restaurateur with Beppi's tenacity and experience could have assembled the ingredients. Even then, it was not easy.

For the *antipasto misto*, a lot of the meats came from a family in St Mary's, friends of Norma's parents who killed their own pig and made their own salami. And there was a Yugoslav butcher at the time, Markovic, who also made salami [he worked for Handler's Smallgoods in Harris Street in Pyrmont]. The basil in the *trenette al pesto Genovese* came from Norma's mother's garden—they also knew several Italian families in the suburbs who grew herbs and spices, artichokes, fennel ... everything. All the seafood for the *ciuppino* (fish soup) came from the Crisafi brothers, there would have been things like calamari, mussels, vongole—actually pippies, they're bigger and chewy but you take them out of their shell and they give good flavour— rockfish, even sardines and harbour prawns. And the radicchio and fennel in the *insalata* would also have come from Norma's mother's friends. The one difficult thing at that time was that there wasn't much olive oil.

The night of the competition meal—Tuesday 12 March—almost ended in disaster.

Beppi cooking the traditional Friuli hearth-style way, called *fogolar furlan* in the local dialect.

There were six on the judging table, among them Dr Renato Velli, head of Alitalia, Commendatore Beghe, the Italian Ambassador at the time (Conte Renato Della Chiesa d'Isaca) and Evasio Costanzo, the editor of the local Italian language newspaper, *La Fiamma*. In the middle of the dinner, the skies opened.

> What happened that night was that we had a colossal storm. The table of judges was at the southern end of the restaurant, the table against the wall and the water came pouring down from the ceiling—we had so many tablecloths on the floor! We kept serving the meal. Norma was sitting at the counter with water pouring all over her—she was very wet. Luckily there was no water in the kitchen. I can't remember if we were laughing, but you know you can't be happy with water all around you like that. I thought it would have affected their judgment.
>
> They finished their meal and said goodbye. Three weeks later, I was in the kitchen cooking while Arena and Marino were on holiday—and Bob Mazzaroli called me and said 'Commendatore Beghe is outside in a car and he wants to talk to you'. I went outside and he gave me the wonderful news that we had won the award. It was fantastic because I didn't think we could win after such a disaster.
>
> There had apparently been an argument between the judges—two of the judges wanted another restaurant to win, while the other four were voting for us. But we won. After that, the promotion for Alitalia coming to Sydney started up, and we began to be very, very busy.

Beppi's determination to provide the people of Sydney with authentic Italian food was beginning to pay off in a spectacular way. From 1963 to the end of the '60s (and beyond), Beppi's was the hot ticket in town. The takings book tells the story. In 1957, takings were around £280 a week; by 1959, they'd gone up to £380; in 1961, £598; by 1965, takings were exceeding £1100 a week. The customers came and they loved it.

> I remember sometimes we were so busy, we'd hand out the bill with the coffee. We had queues outside. It was fantastic. We worked together like a team. Victor Alexander was a great fellow, very good at jokes and with a pleasing manner. Aldo also was very pleasant, he could get away with anything. People used to say, 'It's a pleasure to watch the way you all work'.

In 1964 there was one major change in the kitchen. Giuseppe Arena left and Marino Gullo took over as head chef.

> Arena and Marino didn't get on in the kitchen. Marino left and went to work as a bricklayer. After three weeks, he asked if he could have his job back, and I said, 'Yes', and asked Arena to let him do his job and to leave him alone. Marino was very good, he absorbed the work. Then in 1964, Arena decided to take a holiday in Italy so I put Marino on the stoves. It only took me three months to teach him everything, he was a quick learner. Then Arena came back after six months and asked for his job back. Marino said, 'If you take him back, I'll leave'. So I made the decision to tell Arena, 'I'm sorry, I don't have a job for you any more'. He was very upset.

Beppi's runs very differently to those restaurants where the chef is king or queen. The direction and the style of the food is dictated by the proprietor. This is a system that has operated for many years in Europe and in a few of Sydney and Melbourne's older restaurants.

> No chef here changes anything. I change things. That is a fact. When we decided about dishes, Marino and I talked. We tested it and we said a little more of this, a little less of that. He was very good, he followed my instructions very well. We had such a respect for each other, he never did anything without asking my opinion first. He stayed for thirty-four years.

By the late '60s the menu had begun to take the shape it retained throughout the next decade. First on the list were appetisers. Then followed oysters, mussels, soups, pasta, fish, mixed dishes, steak, poultry, cheese, side salads and sweets, and an inserted sheet of specials, the produce for which was also presented at the table. And right from the beginning there was an abundant display of fresh and seasonal produce and seafood to greet customers at the front door—a tradition that Beppi had imported from the great Italian restaurants.

A sprinkling of standards which even back in the late '60s included *osso buco Milanese*, *cervello Anna Capri* (brains sautéed with capers, wine and parsley

Right: The front cover of the menu from Beppi's displaying the Golden Fork. The original menus with insignia were lino cuts on leather done by Beppi himself.

REEN or BLACK ITALIAN OLIVES
ALAME ITALIANO
ATE MAISON (home made)
RAWN COCKTAIL (cocktail sauce)
NTIPASTO MISTO (hors d'oeuvres varie...
ROSCIUTTO e MELONE (Ita... mo... ser... h rock melon)

50.
40.
80.
80.
80.

	Doz.	½ Doz
YSTERS NATURAL (cockt... sauc...	1.40	5
RIED OYSTERS (egged, cr...mbed...	1.60	1.0

Entre...
$1.1...

USSELS alla MARINARA

INESTRONE (Italian ve...bl...
ISO in BRODO (clear...s...ou...
TRACCIATELLA ROM... (...ie... ou... ... ... up

50.
50.
60.

	Entree	Dinne...
ANELLONI (rolled past... ...ed v... ...cia... and ...t, bak... with gr... chee...	90¢	1.5
ASAGNE VERDI al FORT... ...baked g... ...asta)	90¢	1.5
PAGHETTI alla CARBONA... ...am cheese and ... ...uce)	90¢	1.3
PAGHETTI MARINARA (sea...	90¢	1.5
AVIOLI PIEMONTESE (bologna... ...au...	80¢	1.4
PAGHETTI BOLOGNESE (meat sau...	70¢	1.3
PAGHETTI alla GENOVESE (fre... ...ast...u...	80¢	1.4

RITTO MISTO (mixed fried fish, tartar... sauce)
ILLET of JOHN DORY LIVORNAISE
               (fresh tomato and white wine sauce)
ALAMARI FRITTI (fried fillets of squid, tartare sauce)
ILLET of JOHN DORY MEUNIERE (butter and lemon sauce)

1.9...
2.0...
2.0...
2....

MIXED DISHES

SCALOPPE of VEAL al CARCIOFO (slices of veal, cooked with
                heart of artichokes)
EAL al PROSCIUTTO (chopped ham and fresh cream sauce)
CALOPPINE alla PARMIGIANA (veal crumbed in parmesan cheese)
EAL au BEURRE (veal ...oked with butter and parsley sauce)
RIED CRUMBED LAM...BR... egged, crumbed and fr...)
CALOPPINE al MARSALA (veal ...ed with marsal... wine)
HICKEN LIVERS al ROSMARI... ...fl...ou...
EAL ESCALOPPE CACCIA... ...aut... with ...room... ...d red wine)
OIN of PORK SICILIAN... ...ic... of che... ... and white wine)
EAL SORENTINA (slices of veal with an egg plant sauce)
SSO BUCO MILANESE (veal shank cooked with a white wine and
               mushroom sauce, served with rice)

"Beppi's"

sauce) and *trippa alla Romana* (tripe with sautéed mushrooms, wine and tomato), and a selection of seasonal and regional specials: *fagioni alla Beppi* (hung pheasant braised in red wine with orange zest and juniper berries); *cotechino con polenta* (a long and slow-cooked pork sausage that makes use of all the otherwise unused parts of the pig); and *maiale alla Siciliana* (pork neck with fresh tomatoes, oregano and wine). Perhaps the most interesting thing about these menus is that they could just as easily be presented today, another example of the wisdom of adopting regional and seasonal Italian food and, to a great extent, ignoring fashion. In this way, Beppi was continuing what Alan Davidson, in his *The Oxford Companion to Food* (1999) noted, was 'the Italian tradition of maintaining traditions'. Perhaps it is this reliance on the tried and true that endears Italian food to the world today.

> Why has this place been such a success? Maybe because we could produce such a fantastic variety of dishes. Arena helped me first, then Marino. It has to do also with being born in the game, being dedicated and loving it. You learn because you pick up things in life. For instance, way back, when I worked in Milan and Florence, we'd play cards and drink lambrusco after service and the arguments between chefs and waiters would only be about food. Then in the winter, we'd do the same thing at home, always talking about food. You live in the game.

In October 1966, Beppi took part in the much publicised and hugely successful Italy promotion run jointly by the department store David Jones and Alitalia. In addition to the importation of Italian men's and women's fashions, contemporary art and a life-size reproduction of Michelangelo's statue of *David* (which caused a considerable stir in sixties Sydney), there were a series of lunches featuring four chefs from Sydney's now very popular Italian restaurants: Ettore Prossimo from Buona Sera; Gianni Batista from Grotto Capri; Emilia Catania from Vesuvio; and Beppi Polese. For his lunch for a party of 300 people, Beppi cooked:

> *Zuppa alla Pavese* (clear broth, raw egg, toast and grated cheese)
> *Vitello al carciofo* (veal with artichoke hearts)
> *Zabaglione*

THE TIMES
1976

IN 1976 ISRAELI COMMANDOS ATTACKED UGANDA'S ENTEBBE
AIRPORT AND FREED 103 HOSTAGES. THE CIVIL WAR ENDED
IN LEBANON. AMERICA CELEBRATED ITS BICENTENNIAL AND
JIMMY CARTER WAS ELECTED PRESIDENT. THE SUMMER
OLYMPICS WERE HELD IN MONTREAL. AIR FRANCE AND
BRITISH AIRWAYS BEGAN COMMERCIAL SUPERSONIC FLIGHTS
ON THE CONCORDE.

The wildly popular Swedish pop group, ABBA, toured Australia, holding concerts in Sydney and Melbourne.

On 10 June, the headline in *The Sydney Morning Herald* was '400 block Kerr's car aide hurt'. The previous year's dismissal of Prime Minister Gough Whitlam was still raising temperatures. 1976 also saw a new section in the *Herald*, 'Look!'—the first of their lifestyle sections—under the headline 'spicy tastes of Indonesia' a recipe for satay sauces from Sri Owen's 'home book of Indonesian cookery'. In *The Sunday Herald* on 13 June, a full page 'guide to good living' with restaurateur Johnnie Walker offered recipes for *coq au vin* and *boeuf bourguignon*. A nearby advertisement for Jacob's Creek 1973 claret told us that 'some grapes bring out the best in others'. A flatette in Darlinghurst was advertised at $10 a week (Australia had switched to decimal currency on 14 February 1966). A three-bedroom flat in Point Piper with views of the harbour was $95,000. Jetabout Travel advertised travel to Europe from $1221. Films being shown included *Taxi Driver, Three Days of the Condor* and *The Story of O*. On television, people in Australia were watching 'This is your life' and 'Countdown'.

WINNER OF THE
1963
GOLDEN FORK
AWARD

Above: Beppi standing next to the display table and various awards at the entrance to the restaurant in 1980.

Above: The 'Galloping Gourmets' Len Evans and Graham Kerr, with Beppi in the cellar room in 1967.

Above: Beppi with his head chef, Marino Gullo, and waiter, Gianni Galeo, after winning the Golden Fork for the sixth time, in 1978.

The big time and a big mistake

There was one important change in the 1970s in the world of restaurants—regular food pages in the newspapers. Ted Moloney wrote a column called 'Good Living' in *The Sunday Herald*, elsewhere Graham Kerr and Len Evans wrote on food and wine, and it was the beginning of regular restaurant reviews. Two of the most influential reviewers were 'Sam Orr', the pseudonym of the reviewer for *The Nation Review*, Richard Beckett, a notoriously harsh and intemperate reviewer, and the suave and ultimately hugely influential Sydney advertising man, Leo Schofield, who, in 1975, had published the first edition of his *Eating Out In Sydney* and was writing on food and restaurants in *The Sunday Telegraph*. Schofield went on to become the major reviewer for *The Sydney Morning Herald*, Good Living, which expanded into to a food and wine section in 1982—until he stopped reviewing restaurants for the Fairfax newsgroup in 1993.

Beppi's was the subject of a typically scathing and violent review from Sam Orr in the early 1970s, in which he lashed out at the food, the service and anything else that got in his way. A careful reading of this curiously dissenting opinion uncovers a possible reason. Mr Beckett was known to like a drink, and it was not unknown for him—by his own admission—to over-imbibe while he was eating a meal in a restaurant that he was to review.

This appears to have been the case at Beppi's. 'For some reason', he wrote, 'the waiters decided I was not drinking wine and wouldn't give me any and my business manager had to snatch the wine bottle off an adjacent table to refill the glasses'. It is easy to reconstruct the ugly scene. An increasingly tired and emotional diner's incessant demands for wine are politely ignored by the perennially professional waiters at Beppi's—attempts at persuading him to drink water prove useless, until his male companion (also perhaps the worse for wear) grabs a bottle of wine from diners at an adjacent table (it's a wonder a brawl didn't break out) and they proceed to guzzle it. This would not have been well received and as a form of retribution he lashes out in a review headlined: 'BEPPI CAN STUFF HIS ARTICHOKES …'

Beppi framed the review, and hung it under the Golden Fork with the added instruction: 'WE SAY—SAM ORR CAN STUFF HIS OWN!' Game, set and match to Italy.

Beppi has little to say about reviewers or their reviews, good or bad. Over fifty years, he's seen them come—and go.

> I have no opinion of these reviewers. I had one bad review from Sam Orr. Somebody said, 'Why don't you sue the bastard?' I said, 'What for?' Normally reviewers write such reviews to launch themselves—they write because they want to make it interesting for the public.

Mr Schofield was kinder. While bemoaning the fact that Beppi's had recently closed for lunch (of which more later) he reported, in the 1976 *Eating Out Guide to Sydney* that his dinner 'late last year … was a delight. Beautiful food, first-rate service and a charming atmosphere … the Fettucine [sic] continues splendid. In winter the Cotechino is great. When fresh, the artichokes are stunning … All the fish dishes are fine.' His only gripe is 'The wine list remains impressive and expensive …' but, he concludes with a shrug, 'Life is short'. Beppi's having 'no time' for reviewers does not mean that he lets them get away with what he sees as ignorant or unjust criticism. There are many editors and journalists around town who have felt the sharp edge of Signor Polese's tongue after their trenchant criticism caused by what he saw at the time as their ignorance or arrogance.

By now Beppi's was one of the major drawcards in town. As well as being the lunch and dining spot of choice for the local advertising, media and business fraternity, if you were celebrated, rich, famous—even infamous—you came to Beppi's. A flick through the visitor's book is eye-opening. Royalty, both hereditary and of the stage, screen and concert hall are sprawled across its pages. From Romano Mussolini, a jazz pianist and the son of the man who caused so many problems for Beppi, to Jerry Lewis, for whom waiter Bob Mazzaroli provided some amusement. 'Bob looks like Dean Martin', Beppi explains, 'so when Jerry Lewis came, I said to him, "Wait here, I have someone to show you", and I called Bob out. Jerry Lewis looked shocked'. As well he might—they had broken up somewhat acrimoniously as a partnership in 1956.

In 1974, Gough Whitlam—still Prime Minister—is on the page opposite cabaret singer Frances Fay; jazz pianist and composer Dave Brubeck over the page from the card of Prince Hiro of Japan: 'They wouldn't let him sign the book' Beppi recalls. And Frank Sinatra, whose 1974 visit to Beppi's was noted by

The Daily Telegraph columnist Jim McDougall: 'Don't know how the combined media crews missed this one! Frank Sinatra and 14 friends … made a snap decision on Monday night to dine at Beppi's where they spooned up the straciatella Romana [sic] and forked spaghetti and chicken cacciatore … he signed Beppi's book before he left—"Dear Beppi, just like home buona fortuna Frank Sinatra".' This must have been one of the more pleasant moments of what was for Sinatra a somewhat turbulent time in Sydney. Which makes Norma and Marc's later encounter with him in Las Vegas even more interesting. As she tells the story, 'We went to Caesar's Palace to see him not long after when Marc was thirteen or fourteen, we were only about four rows from the front. At the end of the concert, Marc went up to the stage and said, "Mr Sinatra, you've been to my father's restaurant". "Which restaurant was that?", asked Sinatra. "Beppi's in Sydney", said Marc. And Sinatra said, "I remember it and I'll be back"'. This was highly unlikely. So outraged was the Sydney union movement at Sinatra's portrayal of the local media as 'bums, parasites and buck and a half hookers', they boycotted him and he was stuck in his hotel room with his entourage for three days, unable to leave town. A return to Beppi's *stracciatella alla Romana*, as delicious as it might have been, would have been doubtful.

Although the *stracciatella* was definitely there on the menus of the 1970s, as were other indications of the timelessness of the menu at Beppi's, there were changes. One of those was the *saltimbocca alla Beppi*. The original of this dish, *saltimbocca alla Romana*—'saltimbocca' means leap in the mouth—is an Italian classic: flattened escalopes of veal rolled around a sage leaf and a slice of prosciutto, fried gently in butter, and finished with white wine.

> One of the times Marino was off on holidays I was in the kitchen. Aldo came in and said, 'They want cheese with the saltimbocca'—there's no cheese in a saltimbocca. I said, 'They want cheese, let's give it to them'. We rolled the veal, sage and prosciutto and added asiago cheese.

The duckling *lago di garda* of the '60s had metamorphosed into *duckling alla Beppi* in the '70s. 'We called it lago di garda because it sounded good and ducks swim in lakes.' *Duckling alla Beppi* was braised with red wine, brandy, orange juice and black olive sauce.

A story headlined 'Beppi's 14th Birthday' appeared in June 1970 in the 'Goings on About Town' column in the *Telegraph*. In it, the un-by-lined writer reminisces that 'If my memory serves me correctly, it was at Beppi's I ate, for the first time in a restaurant, mussels and squid. Today, these dishes are fairly common and mussels at Beppi's are superb'. Beppi is quoted as saying 'Without Norma, this restaurant would not be celebrating its 14th birthday now … We have extended the restaurant to seat 150 … and Norma spends her 16 hours a day looking after Marc'.

Just before Christmas in 1975, Beppi made his first bad decision: to close for lunch. The downside of being so busy is working impossible hours, and they were taking their toll.

Marino was working sixteen hours a day, I was working sixteen hours a day. There was a stretcher at the back of the restaurant and we would grab a couple of hours sleep when we could. At that time, Aldo and Bob Mazzaroli left. I was so tired when I walked home at night, I could hardly make it up the stairs. Then I'd fall into bed, boom! Asleep immediately. And back then, I was also doing the markets every morning. I tried to talk Aldo into staying until January, but his mind was made up. So I thought the best thing to do was to close for lunch. What I should have done is looked for another chef. I lost a lot of customers during that time. Before I closed I had about 700 business accounts—I didn't take cards then, and used to send out the bills every month. When we re-opened in 1976, the year American Express came to Australia, I joined. But it took me two or three years to build up the business again. It was so quiet I used to go up to Chianti at lunchtime for a coffee with my friend Franco Orsati. Also when I re-opened I hired Tony Biondi as a chef, which is what I should have done before.

Right: Beppi and his restaurant manager, Aldo Zuzza, in the main dining room of Beppi's in 1976.

THE TIMES
1986

IN APRIL 1986 THERE WAS A MAJOR NUCLEAR ACCIDENT AT
CHERNOBYL POWER STATION. PRESIDENT MARCOS WAS OUSTED
IN THE PHILIPPINES AND FLED THE COUNTRY. ARGENTINA WON
THE WORLD CUP BEATING WEST GERMANY. HALLEY'S COMET
REAPPEARED IN 1985 AND 1986 FOR THE FIRST TIME SINCE 1910.

On 10 June the headline in *The Sydney Morning Herald* was 'Unsworth's
machine grinds into power'. With the resignation of Premier Neville Wran,
Barry Unsworth was the heir apparent. An accompanying story told of a
meeting between Unsworth and his wife Pauline with Australian Labor Party
powerbroker John McBean and his wife Gail at the Sydney Hilton, where they
ate sizzler burgers and drank Wolf Blass Riesling rather than Neville Wran's
tipple of choice, Rosemount Chardonnay—he had decided to quit while
drinking the Rosemount.

The Lindy Chamberlain enquiry was in full swing with a story in
The Daily Mirror headlined 'Dingos were hungry'. Also in the *Mirror*,
'Restaurants feel the tax pinch—lunches down 50 per cent'. The story
reported that Pierre Flaco of Le Provençal Restaurant was closing down
and heading to Tahiti.

A three-bedroom house in Rose Bay was $395,000. A five-bedroom
house with 'panoramic views' in the same suburb was $1,050,000.
A three- to four-bedroom house in Rose Bay was to let at $300 a week.

On television Australians were watching 'Reilly Ace of Spies',
'Neighbours', 'The Two Ronnies' and 'Dynasty'; at the movies, *Crocodile
Dundee*, *Hannah and Her Sisters* and *9½ Weeks*.

Since 15 June 1982, the *Herald* had been publishing a food and wine section every Tuesday called 'Good Living', taking the name from *The Sunday Herald* pages written by Johnnie Walker and Ted Moloney.

On Tuesday, 3 June 1986, the lead story, by Meg Jamieson, was on 'Sydney's Little Italys', in which Ms Jamieson identified 15 Italian regions whose cuisine was represented in Sydney—a remarkable roll call in just twenty years. Beppi's was listed as representing the cuisine of the recently created region of Friuli-Venezia Giulia, the recipe cited *quaglie di campo con polenta* (marinated quail with sage, rosemary, bacon and white wine served with polenta). Aldo Zuzza, now at Darcy's, represented the Veneto (having ceded Friuli-Venezia Giulia to his senior) and nominated *carpaccio*.

On the same page, Elizabeth King took readers on a tour of Italian wine regions and elsewhere cookery writer Elise Pascoe helped identify and obtain such Italian ingredients as olive oil, *coppa, prosciutto crudo, mascarpone*—many of them still as hard to find as they were ten years earlier.

This was also the decade that witnessed the birth of that difficult to define and often even more difficult to swallow cuisine 'Modern Australian' or 'ModOz', Australia's own contribution to the twentieth century's attempts to 'modernise' cuisine, which began (according to Larousse Gastronomique) in 1972. ModOz was short lived, being dropped from the categories listed in the *Herald's Good Food Guide* in 2006 (replaced by 'Contemporary'). This movement also gave rise in Sydney to what was known to some commentators as the 'Temples of Gastronomy', restaurants where newly emerging celebrity chefs ruled supreme and dictated to management and customers alike. This was not how things were run at Beppi's—firstly, remember Beppi's emphatic statement, 'No chef here changes anything. I change things'; and secondly, such occurrences as the invention of *saltimbocca alla Beppi*: 'I said, they want cheese, let's give it to them'. A firm hand on the wheel and the customer is always right are two of the rules that have kept Beppi's open and prospering for fifty years.

Thirty years on

Beppi stays true to tradition in the age of ModOz.
Weathering the Fringe Benefits Tax

The Fringe Benefits Tax (FBT), one of a whole series of tax reforms introduced by the Keating Government in July 1986, was a tax on benefits provided to employees other than salary. Its effect was to make it very difficult for businesspeople to write off entertaining—taking clients to lunch, and so on—as tax deductions. Beppi shrugged it off. 'At the time, I was very worried about it. I told the staff we had to tighten our belts. Then, the next year [1987] was one of the best years we had.'

He maintains that his adherence to his roots—region and seasonal Italian food—stood him in good stead during all the hard times, recessions and FBT included. He had and has little time for 'contemporary' cuisine, emphasising that what Italians ate in Italy reflected what was essentially a reflection of limited available options.

> Trying to modernise Italian food is impossible because Italian food is founded on regional food and every region has its own dishes. Traditionally, people cooked the things they'd grow themselves, depending on how well off they were and how much land they had, whether one cow or two cows, one pig or two pigs, how many chickens they had. The animals gave food for the family. The animals also ate what was grown. And that controlled what you cooked. You can't cook what you can't grow.
>
> But why is there such variety in Italian food? To answer that question you must go back into history. The Romans brought back slaves from the countries they fought and occupied—Gauls, Arabs, Africans. The influence of the Arab countries on Italian cooking is phenomenal. They brought their culinary knowledge with them and this was absorbed. Later, Napoli was occupied by the Spanish, the north-east by the Austrians and the north by the French. They added to the mix. But then the other way, the Romans

were also a huge influence. Wherever they went, they built baths, aqueducts, grew grapevines—and their food.

In the meantime, the reviews continued to be positive. Back in 1980, a now repentant Sam Orr wrote in his review of Beppi's in his restaurant guide, *Hungry Eye* (1980), 'Some years ago I went to Beppi's, had an awful meal and spent about a thousand and a half words spreading them all over the face of a newspaper that no longer matters. Beppi's responded with equal viciousness. They pinned up my review under their restaurant Golden Fork of the Year award. Everyone had a good laugh. I still maintain they serve hot mineral water but I will agree that they do Italian things much better than any restaurant in Sydney'. He continued on in a complimentary manner before finishing with 'But it is not cheap. To dine there properly will cost you at least $40 for two people and perhaps quite a lot more'.

By 1984, the *Good Food Guide* was edited by Leo Schofield (with David Dale and Jenna Price). The review of Beppi's is interesting enough to quote in full:

Beppi Polese has watched Sydney grow from a hick town to a multicultural society—at least as far as its food tastes go. When he opened his restaurant in 1956, no Sydneysider would eat calamari or mussels. His persistence with our taste buds has been rewarded—and now he's a wealthy man. But you'll still find him in the restaurant, trying to interest diners in yet another regional speciality. The printed menu here offers a range of heavy classics for business lunches, but the adventurous should listen for specials like cotechino (a kind of salami served hot) with beans, horseradish and polenta (an ancient dumpling which the Ancient Romans took to Britain and turned into Yorkshire pudding); or fettucine with broccoli, anchovies and a little chilli. Beppi carries his innovation through to desserts, of which the poached pear and zabaglione is the pinnacle. Beppi's is still one of Sydney's best Italian restaurants.

Aside from the continued misspelling of 'fettuccine', and the alarming assertion that polenta is a dumpling which, somehow, metamorphosed into Yorkshire pudding, what the reviewer seems not to have noticed was that polenta had been on the menu at least since the late '60s—with the *cotechino* and the tripe—

Beppi at the restaurant in the 1970s.

and such (then) exotic dishes as *spaghetti nero di seppie veneziana*—squid ink pasta with cuttlefish strips.

In the Australian bicentenary year of 1988, the reviewer in the *Good Food Guide,* now edited by Leo Schofield and Michael Dowe, asserted that 'Beppi's just keeps on keeping on. Is it possible that like a good wine it actually gets better with age? After 31 years [Beppi's] is a Sydney institution ... unreservedly recommended, for business or pleasure'. As in 1984, it had been awarded one chef's hat [out of a maximum of three].

The review in '88 also made mention of the Polese farm in Orchard Hills, bought in 1964, which they still own, although it was leased out in 2005.

> Over the years we turned it into an oasis. We planted 1000 trees a year, eventually planting 10,000—we had plums, peaches, nectarines, grapes, kiwi fruit. We grew all our own greens and herbs for the restaurant and there was a distillery up there. We were making grappa using the must from muscatel table grapes. We don't make it any more, but we still have 3000 litres.

Beppi became involved in another venture in the 1980s. In addition to running a restaurant and a farm, he was an active partner in opal mines in Coober Pedy (in outback South Australia) and Lightning Ridge (in central New South Wales) and can talk at length and with expert knowledge on the different techniques for mining opals in each region.

THE TIMES
1996

IN 1996 FRANCE AGREED TO END NUCLEAR TESTING. BRITAIN WAS ALARMED BY THE OUTBREAK OF MAD COW DISEASE. THE TALIBAN SEIZED KABUL. APPROXIMATELY 45 MILLION PEOPLE WERE USING THE INTERNET. ELLA FITZGERALD AND MARCELLO MASTROIANNI DIED.

John Howard was sworn in as the twenty-fifth prime minister of Australia on 11 March. The headline in *The Sydney Morning Herald* on 11 June was 'Nearing up for a waterfront war'. Peter Ryan from London, the new head of the New South Wales police force, began work that week: 'Nice bloke but is he mongrel enough?', the headline.

The Sunday Telegraph notes, 'thousands of guns handed in' after the Port Arthur massacre and 'renters now pay half weekly wages'.

A three-bedroom unit in Darlinghurst was for sale at $295,000. A three-bedroom house in Randwick, $450,000. At the movies we watched *Trainspotting*, *The Birdcage* and *Twister*. *Braveheart*, the Mel Gibson film, won the Oscar for Best Picture.

The fortieth anniversary of Beppi's is recorded in the column 'Short Black' in the *Herald*, which noted that it was a place where 'everybody was welcome, not just the silvertails'. The cover story in the section 'Good Living' that day was '25 hottest cafés'. Terry Durack was the new restaurant reviewer.

Forty years later. A new restaurant

In January 1992, Mezzaluna had opened. Beppi, Marc and Norma tell the story.

Beppi: Norma and I had eaten at Butler's restaurant on Victoria Street on several occasions—it was a beautiful building with views out to the city and Saint Mary's Cathedral. A customer at Beppi's, Joseph Brender, owned it and Norma asked me to ask him if he wanted to sell it. Norma always had eyes for real estate. He agreed to sell it and we bought it in 1984.

Butler's, the restaurant, was then run by influential chef Mogens Bay Esbensen and Joyce Johnson. The building is on the edge of the cliff that drops down to the old harbourside suburb of Woolloomooloo. The dining room faced west with spectacular views across Woolloomooloo Bay to the city skyline.

Marc: Mum always thought that because Beppi's was a company title building, if enough people wanted to sell it, to a developer, for instance, we'd be out. So she thought we ought to have another site like the one in Victoria Street to move into, just in case.

At that time I was working as a vet in Orange, then I moved back to Sydney, did an internship in Veterinary clinical studies and sat for membership of the College of Small Animal Surgeons and worked in the Crows Nest Veterinary Hospital from 1988 to 1991. In 1991, Butler's closed and we tried to lease the place out. Then mum said she'd really like to gut it and renovate it and that she had the perfect name for it. Dad said we need another restaurant like we need a hole in the head and I had my career to consider, but having grown up here [in the restaurant] it's in your blood—I can't imagine life without it.

But then again, I didn't think our family, with me being an only child, needed another business like that. So what we thought was we'd renovate it, do it up and operate it and sell it as a going concern—which would make it easier to sell. So we spent six months renovating.

Norma: I thought 'Mezzaluna' was a beautiful name (it means half moon in Italian, and is also the name given to a curved, usually two-handled mincing knife). We used an Italian interior designer, Dino Raccanello. It was a great joy to me to refurbish it and get the artworks together—all those depictions of the mezzaluna opposite the bar. I just loved creating that place, and I still love it today. Having put it together, we couldn't possibly sell it.

Marc: I gave up my veterinarian career from 1992 to 1994 and worked there with mum. After we got it going I began to think—if I don't do some vetting, all that study and hard work will go down the drain. So now I practise every Monday at Crows Nest Veterinary Hospital.

Norma: I heard someone once say—tongue in cheek—we won't have the *osso buco*, Marc's here today …

But the two restaurants are very different.

Norma: Beppi's is more traditional and regional. It's warm, cosy, it's got older Italian waiters, it hasn't got a view. Mezzaluna is open, airy, with sensational views, younger waiters, and the food is more contemporary. We didn't want to create competition for Beppi's, we wanted an alternative—you can go to Beppi's one night and Mezzaluna another and experience different styles of Italian food and atmosphere.

The 1993 *Good Food Guide*—the last to be edited by Leo Schofield and Michael Dowe—awarded Mezzaluna a star for 'extra sparkle', and announced that 'This is probably the best looking modern restaurant in Sydney' but that 'Not unexpectedly the food has a bit of a problem living up to these swagger surroundings and possibly also the expectations of the owner, veteran restaurateur Beppi Polese. However, after a hiccupy start with revolving chefs, the food has settled down to be highly acceptable with a Mediterranean flavour'. Not a mention of Norma or Marc, who ran it and whose creation it was.

By 2003, Beppi's had reached the shape it has today. The last change was the addition of a private room at the very back, the Magnum Room, the only area in the restaurant with a closing door. It is where, for example, the Labor Party heavyweights Bob Carr, Paul Keating, John Faulkner and Gareth Evans lunched on 2 May 2006, as reported in the CBD Column in the *Herald* business section the following day. (We have no idea what they discussed behind that closed door, but we do know that Mr Keating ate marinated mushrooms, drank one glass of wine and then switched to mineral water.) It is perhaps fitting that there is a sign in Italian hanging on the wall of this room which reads: *A tavola non ci sono nemici* (there are no enemies at the table).

Beppi's has gradually grown bigger over the years. In 1962, when the building transferred to company title, the Poleses bought the restaurant they had, until then, rented. In 1967, they bought the grocery store north of the existing restaurant, and then helped the barber shop next door move to leave space for an extra room—on the right as you walk in the front door. Then, over the years, an old air-raid shelter at the back of the restaurant was bought which now houses the kitchen, preparation and storage rooms, then more units at the rear of the building, which now house the small maze of cellar rooms lined with wine bottles, as well as storage and staff rooms. In the largest of these is Professor Bissietta's second fresco, with its dog Latin inscription *Tofontanelus alias Bissietta Miniatensis pinait*, which identified him as being from San Miniato, near Florence.

Of course the décor has changed over the years. The first incarnation of the restaurant featured red check tablecloths and Chianti bottles with candles, the style of the '50s. But in a piece in the *Sun-Herald* in 1975, Johnnie Walker noted that 'for his first décor he practised the Italian custom of hanging his cheeses and salamis from the ceiling. Today these are gone and the vastly enlarged premises are rather elegant'. It was noted in the article on Beppi's fourteenth birthday that the restaurant then (1970) seated 150, although Beppi says that it holds no more than 130.

The next major change of décor was in 1994, when the still relatively new reviewer from Melbourne, Terry Durack, noted the 'recent facelift' and 'apricot coloured walls'. The book *Wogfood* noted 'a smart black awning outside, and large windows let into the front'. The same change introduced a modernised logo, which is now being phased out in preference for the script that was used in the '60s and '70s.

Beppi's received a major review in 'Good Living' in 1994 from Terry Durack. The review opened with a homage to the restaurant's longevity.

'Where to?'
'Yurong Str ...'
'Ah, Beppi's.'
That's the best thing about going to lunch at Sydney's oldest family-owned restaurant. The taxi drivers know exactly where it is.

While Mr Durack enjoyed his meal overall, he found the polenta 'too salty to provide much comfort', the salt cod not salty enough, and the desserts 'barely motivational'. One interesting comment was 'I would have been hellishly unhappy with the meal of scallop mornay and gratinated crab that was lapped up and seemingly enjoyed at the next table'.

It was the era of culinary invention, of fusion food, and the traditional comfort food served at Beppi's was no longer enough for such reviewers. In this difficult decade, novelty, not fidelity, was rewarded. It is worth noting that most of the 'hot new' restaurants of the '90s are no longer with us. Beppi's policy of caring more for his customers than the critics is a recipe for longevity, and success. And his food, as always, is and was—Italian.

> The Italians always had the basics of cooking from ancient times. If they changed things, they did so from an understanding of their cooking methods. When I added cheese to *saltimbocca*, for example, I was changing an existing dish. The young chefs here think they are champions—they do a four-year apprenticeship. I did eight, and I worked in so many different places and picked up so much knowledge. In Australia, we have the same thing happening in food as when the Romans began adding outside influences, but here, they don't have the foundations, it's as if they're building a house and they start from the roof.

A different, irreverent but respectful view of Beppi's was offered by Catherine Keenan in her column 'Eatstreets' in the *Sun-Herald* on 22 April 2001. 'This used to be the place for an impressive business lunch ... and nothing has changed in the decades Beppi's has been running. Why mess with a winning formula? There's a fantastic cellar where you can eat surrounded by dust-covered wine bottles; the old waiters are loads of fun; and the Italian fare is a good notch or two above the

Left: The 'rather elegant' restaurant, Beppi's, that Johnnie Walker reviewed for *Sun-Herald* readers in 1975.

average (as it should be—prices are high). Especially good was the veal saltimbocca with just the right amount of sage, and the super rich pasta shells filled with veal, ricotta and tomato'.

The glaring error in this review is 'used to be a place for an impressive business lunch'. It was—ask for the table where Sir Peter Abeles nutted out the details of the purchase of Ansett Transport Industries with Sir Reg Ansett over, perhaps, a *saltimbocca alla Beppi*—and still is. Leo Schofield reports seeing 'Rupert Murdoch, James Fairfax and a dozen other heavies' there. At the time of writing, on a Wednesday afternoon in the August of 2006, the joint, as the saying goes, is jumping. Both rooms and the cellars are packed. A table of chic French-speaking Africans are enjoying their meal. Nearby, two twenty-first century entrepreneurs in jeans and T-shirts do a deal over a bottle of the Henschke Cyril. In the main room, seasoned suits huddle over their wine and seafood, and a table of young women corporates—not born when Beppi's opened—noisily celebrate a victory. So busy was the restaurant that day, Marc Polese is on the floor helping out. Beppi is bemused, but not surprised, that after fifty years, he's still packing them in. There have been slow periods—you would expect them over fifty years—but even so, they keep coming back.

Three or four times in the past it has slowed down. They go away for two or three months. But they always come back. We forget one important thing. The way human beings are made. When you eat something, it's a sensation for the palate, you must taste it. Flavour is the thing. That's what it's all about—it makes you feel good. My food is still attractive. And that's why they keep coming back. I tell the kitchen—flavour, flavour, flavour—then sometimes they put in too much flavour!

Right: Natalie Boag's portrait of Beppi which came second in a *Sydney Morning Herald* portrait competition in 2005. **Next page:** The second of two frescos commissioned by Italian artist, Professor Bissietta, which adorns one of the labyrinthine dining rooms at Beppi's.

The Golden Fork dinner

ANTIPASTO MISTO

For the Golden Fork dinner in 1963, we used the best prosciutto (sliced thin) and the best salami (sliced thicker) we could find—although neither were what I had known in Italy—and served them with olives, anchovies and *Insalata Russa* (Russian salad). That is boiled potatoes and carrots cut into small cubes, with peas, capers, hard-boiled eggs and tiny (shelled) prawns. It's dressed with mayonnaise into which you stir a little powdered English mustard, or, if you prefer, horseradish.

RISTRETTO DI BUE IN TAZZA

The French like to serve sorbet between courses, but I find that too sweet and heavy. I wanted something light and savoury so we served chicken and beef consommé in a cup. You make a clear stock using chicken and beef bones, onion, celery, carrots, thyme and egg shells. Bring it to the boil and add a dash of sherry, then pour it in the cups, and add salt, pepper and a generous dash of sherry to each cup. Sprinkle some small crunchy cubes of bread fried in butter into each cup and serve.

TRENETTE AL PESTO GENOVESE

First make your pesto sauce. For four people you need 6 cups of basil leaves. In the old days the leaves were pounded in a pestle and mortar but now you can put them in a blender or food processor with 3 tablespoons of pine nuts, 4 cloves of chopped garlic, ½ cup of grated parmesan, ½ cup of grated hard pecorino and 1 cup of extra virgin olive oil.

Blend for 10 seconds and taste to see if it needs more of any ingredient before blending again. Don't add salt until you've tasted it, because sometimes pecorino can be salty. I like to add a pinch of cayenne pepper because it balances the fattiness of the oil. You can also blend in a boiled potato if you want to thicken the sauce and reduce the saltiness.

(You can keep pesto in the fridge for months, provided it's in a sealed glass jar with olive oil on top of the sauce.)

Trenette are wider and thinner than tagliatelle noodles that you can make yourself (see how my mother did it in chapter 1) or buy at a good deli. If you are using dried pasta, boil for about 10 minutes in a lot of salted water, for fresh pasta about 5 minutes. Drain and toss in a bowl with 50 g of unsalted butter. Spoon the pesto over the pasta, stir it through, and serve in warmed bowls with extra grated parmesan.

Note: Never cook the pesto after it has been mixed with the pasta.

CIUPPINO DI PESCE AL GOLFO DI VENEZIA

They make fish soup all around Italy, under all sorts of names. I first learnt how to do it in Venice, but this is a version from Venezia. The important thing is to make a good fish stock first, using crushed fish bones and heads and lobster shells, simmered for 2 hours with onion, celery, carrots, bay leaves, tarragon, salt and pepper, then strained. You then need to boil the stock with egg shells and reduce it.

You can use all sorts of seafood, but I prefer not to have ingredients that are hard to get the meat from (apart from crab legs, which are more for decoration than for eating). You must clean them carefully, cut them into small pieces and remove as many bones as possible.

I'd suggest a mix of rock fish, squid, cuttlefish, whiting, raw prawns, small mussels, baby clams and blue swimmer crabs. In a big pot, fry some onion, garlic and 4 crushed anchovy fillets in oil for 3 minutes, then add the sliced squid and cuttlefish, cook for 5 minutes, then add all the other seafood with 1 cup of white wine and 1 teaspoon of tarragon. Fry for another 5 minutes to evaporate the alcohol and pour in enough stock to almost cover the seafood. Cover and simmer for another 10 minutes.

Serve with toasted bread that has been rubbed with garlic and splashed with olive oil.

FILLETTO DI BUE ALLA VALDOSTANA

We served the fillet steak fairly simply on the Golden Fork night, but later I improved on the recipe. Slice a whole fillet steak into pieces about 2 cm thick and season them with salt and pepper. Fry 3 pieces per person in butter for about 1 minute, turn them and sprinkle with brandy. On each piece, place a slice of soft cheese (asiago or fontina) and some fresh ground pepper, cover the frying pan and simmer for another 3 minutes. The cheese will partly run into the sauce, which should be poured over the meat when you serve it. That's the 'Valdostana' method.

But the next time we did this dish, it became 'Mignonette al rosemarino'. First you brown the pieces of beef in a frying pan with butter for about 1 minute each side. Sauté a sliced garlic clove and 1 tablespoon of rosemary leaves in some more butter for 1 minute, then put the fillets into the frying pan with a splash of brandy, 1 teaspoon of French mustard, 1 teaspoon of chopped parsley, and 2 shakes of Worcestershire sauce. Simmer everything together for 2 minutes and remove the fillets to a serving dish. Now put 1 tablespoon of cream into the sauce, stir and reduce for 2 minutes, and pour the sauce over the fillets.

Note: Don't reduce the sauce too much, otherwise it breaks down and becomes oily.

POMODORI FARCITI CON RISO

To make stuffed tomatoes, cut the tops off and scrape out the seeds with a teaspoon. Sprinkle the insides of the tomatoes with salt and pepper, and put them upside down to let the liquid drain. Brown a finely chopped onion in butter, then add some rice and stir for a few minutes. Add chicken stock and cook the mixture for 10 minutes. Stir some cheese (asiago or montasio) through the rice with a little butter, fill the tomatoes with the mixture and bake in a 160°C oven for 10 minutes. Add some of the juices from the baking dish and serve.

With the tomatoes we offered beans and sliced carrots that had been simmered in chicken stock and butter, finely sliced zucchini (cougettes) sautéed in butter, and potatoes in little balls, also sautéed in butter.

Also good served with the stuffed tomatoes is a radicchio and fennel salad with oil and vinegar dressing.

TORTA SACRIPANTINA

This is a kind of chocolate cake from Genoa, made with layers of sponge (what we call 'pan di Spagna' in Italy). You could bake a basic sponge, but it's easier to buy one at your local cake shop. Slice it into 3 discs. Place 1 slice on a large plate, sprinkle with marsala, spread sweetened ricotta mixed with cocoa, warm zabaglione (see chapter 4), and *crèma pasticcera*, which is the filling you put inside *profiteroles* (it's made by beating together egg yolks, butter, caster sugar and a little flour). Continue each layer and finish by pouring zabaglione on top and sprinkle with bitter chocolate. When you cut the cake, make sure there's a dob of cream and a cherry on top of each slice.

With the *torta*, we served candied chestnuts and nougat imported from Italy, and with the coffee we served fresh fruit and a bowl of warm water so people could wash their fingers.

CHAPTER SEVEN

A LIFETIME IN HOSPITALITY

Left: Beppi in his restaurant in 1999, when the President of the Italian Republic, Carlo Ciampi, came to dine. The menu that night included antipasto, pasta and wild barramundi.

THE TIMES
2006

IN 2006 THE WAR CONTINUED TO RAGE IN IRAQ. ISRAEL AND HEZBOLLAH CLASHED IN LEBANON IN AUGUST. SADDAM HUSSEIN WAS FOUND GUILTY OF CRIMES AGAINST HUMANITY IN NOVEMBER AND SENTENCED TO HANG. THE INTERNATIONAL HEADLINES CONTINUED TO BE DEPRESSING.

In Australia, John Howard celebrated his tenth year as prime minister.

The headline in *The Sydney Morning Herald* of 12 June, the fiftieth birthday of Beppi's (actually the day after but the 11th was a Sunday), screams 'The time is now', signalling the eve of Australia's first World Cup match against Japan. It was the first time Australia had qualified since 1974.

The story continued, 'a long wait for a sport once considered suitable only for "sheilas wogs and poofters"'. Australia defeated Japan, drew against Croatia, were beaten by Brazil and knocked out by Italy in July.

Meanwhile, the news headline was 'Beazley: I'll demolish PM's poison work contracts' referring to the government's new industrial relation laws.

A one-bedroom unit in Darlinghurst was renting for $330 a week, and a four-bedroom house in Rose Bay was being auctioned for 'about $2 million'.

Among films showing were *Candy*, *Colour Me Kubrick* and *The World's Fastest Indian*. Popular on television were World Cup soccer, 'Arrested Development', 'Commander-in-Chief', and a number of food shows.

By 2006, Sydney is a food aware—some might say obsessed—city. The *Herald*'s Good Living, by now a stand alone food and wine section (without the fashion pages it began with) had as its cover on 13 June 'lights camera pasta'—the

best food moments in film to coincide with the Sydney Film Festival. New reviewer Simon Thomsen liked what he ate at Bird Cow Fish in Surry Hills—among other dishes crisp skinned chicken with braised witlof; cavalo nero fennel and shaved ricotta with a vincotto reduction; ocean trout with tapenade and a beef cheek pie with an 'awesome' sour cream pastry base; finishing with an almond sponge with crema catalana and a single origin macchiato. All of these words and ingredients are perfectly familiar to the readers and offered without explanation.

Cookery writer Bill Granger offered recipes for pasta: pappardelle with porcini, tomato and parsley; gnocchi with gorgonzola, spinach and walnuts and rigatoni with Italian sausage.

The Daily Telegraph's Wednesday food pages led with an article on the world coffee art competition in Berne, Switzerland where an Australian barista was competing and a review of 3 Fat Fish in Manly by reviewer Jeff Collerson.

Wild pigs, and success

Maybe the most remarkable thing about Beppi Polese at 81 is his infectious enthusiasm. For his work, for food, for the restaurant—for life itself. Although he and Norma no longer work at night, they are in their respective restaurants every day, with Beppi greeting and farewelling his army of regulars, encouraging and mentoring staff, and sometimes giving them a hard time if they don't live up to his standards. 'Tearing strips off a staff member' was the answer upon enquiring once, over the phone, where he was.

But get him started on a recipe, why he prefers a pot on the stove top rather than in the oven, how to cook a hung pheasant, what is wrong with modern food, the history of Italian cooking—and you will be talking to someone deeply in love with his subject, and with strong and well-formed views on it.

One such discussion, on pot braising a suckling pig, elicited a story of a pig shooting expedition to Lightning Ridge in the 1980s from Marc.

> We're camping at Lightning Ridge and we killed a suckling pig. Dad skinned, it, gutted it, put the entrails in a bag, handed it to me and said 'go outside and throw these away'. I was about ten at the time. It's pitch black outside the tent and I walk out carrying this bag of pig innards. And then I hear a deep grunting in the darkness—a pig snort. And rustling in the bushes. I went wooooooo!!!!, screaming back into the tent. And said, 'Dad, Dad, there's something out there'. We got out the spotlight and turned it on and we were surrounded by pigs. We got the rifle out and shot at them to scare them off.

Beppi, of course, is more interested in the cooking of the pig.

We pot roasted it. We had olive oil with us, we chopped up an onion, some garlic, celery, potatoes and rosemary, cooked the onion just a little, cut the pig up and put it in the pot with all the other ingredients and a little wine. Then we put the lid on the corner of the pot and put the pot on the coolest part of the fire and went out shooting for three, four hours. We came back, and it was beautiful—it had a fantastic flavour. It's a magnificent way of cooking. Sometimes the simplest thing is the best—I don't like the barbecue—burning the meat spoils the flavour.

Perhaps Beppi's most remarkable achievement in fifty years is to have turned a profit, and for so long. This is no mean feat in a town notorious for its restaurants opening and closing with the frequency of the cool room door in a bottle shop. According to Restaurant & Catering NSW, 300 of their members close each year—and not all restaurants are members. In such an environment, Beppi's has not only stayed open, not only stayed full, but has delivered a profit for almost every one of those fifty years. The secrets behind that success make for fascinating reading.

Waste not.
Making money in a restaurant

You look at my menus. Back when I was charging 80 cents for an entrée, I used tripe, kidneys, liver, chicken thighs, capsicum. There was no expensive ingredients. But those inexpensive ingredients were carefully cooked to give flavour. And nothing was wasted.

To work out what you will charge, you multiply what you buy by four times what it cost you. But then you've got waste. For instance, I've got a fillet of beef that cost me $28 a kilogram. But when it's trimmed, about $5

of that is waste. So we use the trim for ragù bolognese, for beef stock—nothing is wasted, we reduce the cost.

I was supervising the cooking in another restaurant there and a young chef was cutting up celery—he cut off the tops and the bottoms and threw them away—the best bits! Our kitchen is run on the basis of use everything, not much waste.

When we use lobsters and scampi, we remove and wash the heads, then we crush them and use them to make a bisque. We sometimes buy lobster heads that other people haven't used to make fish stock.

The profit in a restaurant starts in the kitchen. It has to. But you have to be careful to get the best price for quality ingredients without sacrificing quality on the plate. And you have to give value according to what you are charging. A lot of places charge a lot and give practically nothing on the plate. Of all the cuisines, Italian is one of the most generous ones, and that should show on the plate.

Italian food is the cuisine of opportunity, born out of poverty. The people working the land kept only the worst and cheapest parts of the food that they grew and raised. They either sold the best, or kept it for festivals. They had no choice but to produce food with flavour using the worst ingredients, that's what happened. That's why you have so much variety and so many standards in Italian cuisine. You can have expensive seafood or a beautiful bowl of pasta that doesn't cost much at all.

The view from the cellar

In 1975, legendary restaurateur Johnnie Walker wrote about a meal at Beppi's:

> Between courses ... he showed me his cellar and quite frankly I was astounded. I have written here about the superb cellars of Maxim's famous restaurant in

Paris. Allowing for the fact that they are a century old, Beppi is catching up fast. He has 28,000 bottles of wine in his reserve bin, the oldest dating back to 1954 (and in this wine-conscious Australia of today, that's not bad going).

At a lunch to celebrate the fortieth birthday of the restaurant, a table of invited journalists finished—in quite short order—a bottle of Chateau d'Yquem, the legendary and pricy dessert wine from Sauternes. Seeing the empty bottle on the table, Beppi disappeared into the cellar and re-appeared with a bottle of the 1966 Yquem. Recognising it as one of the rarest and most expensive of the vintages for this wine (in 2001, a bottle sold for US$800 at auction), one guest mentioned this and asked Beppi whether he wanted to reconsider opening it. There was no pause, the cork was immediately pulled. 'Wine is for drinking', he told the table.

In a city where water views seem essential for success, Beppi's customers have to make do with wine views. The most desirable seats in the house are in a warren of dark, dusty bottle-lined rooms deep in the heart of the building. If Beppi told Johnnie Walker how many bottles his cellar held back then, today he is a little cagier.

A lot of people ask me how many bottles of wine I have in the restaurant. I don't know. But I do know I have 290 vintages. I began collecting seriously in 1959 when we got a licence for the restaurant.

When we bought the unit at the back and we built the cellar rooms with wine racks going up to the ceiling, every dozen bottles of wine I bought, I would put aside the last six bottles. That's how I have built up such a large variety of vintages. Because of that system, I have half a dozen bottles of each vintage.

When Seppelt, Penfolds, Lindeman and Henschke release a vintage, once a year, they give me the list and I go through it and say, 'OK, I want a dozen of this and a dozen of that'. I don't need to taste them. I trust their quality, I know the type of wine. The new labels are attractive, but the old labels are trustworthy. Young people have different opinions, I suppose, but I'm not so keen on the new labels. They produce their wines according to trends—to the taste of the drinkers rather than the tastes of the winemaker.

Being a good cook,
and working with cooks

In fifty years, Beppi's has had just four head chefs. The shortest lived of these was Giuseppe Arena, who began in 1959 and left in 1963. If it had not been for his clash with the next, Marino Gullo (1963–1995), he may well have stayed much longer. Tony Biondi began in the kitchen in 1976 when they re-opened for lunch and when Marino was still there, took over when he left and stayed until 2002, and current chef, Djamel Douadi, began as a commis when Gullo was in charge, and when Biondi left he took over. Also still in the kitchen in charge of cold larder since 1973 is Maria Rimi. That's a considerable achievement for any restaurant, let alone one where the chef appears to play second fiddle to the restaurateur. But that restaurateur has a deep understanding of food and, by his own admission, and with no false modesty, 'a magnificent, natural palate'. For Beppi Polese, it all starts and ends in the kitchen.

When I started I did the menu. I talked to the chef, the chef would cook a dish then give it to me to correct it. Over the years, I've built up their trust because I know what I'm talking about, and they don't question me. Even today, I look in the kitchen and find things to correct. I say to chefs— if you do what I tell you, I might be wrong, but it's my responsibility. Think about that. If you want to be a good cook, you've got to be dedicated and prepared to cop a bit of flak when you make a mistake. You must notice everything that is going on in the kitchen.

And you have to know, first of all, the basics of cooking.

How to treat veal, how to dissect a chicken, how to marinate. An example of that, we produce sun-dried tomatoes, they have my specific flavouring in them. The oil I use to marinate the tomatoes is the oil I use for marinating scampi. And what you have created is something unique because it is made using something that you have preserved.

If you have an instinctive understanding of cooking, you make connections with flavours. For instance, when we cook prawns and scampi, all seafood, we boil them one after the other in the same fish stock. At the end, that base stock has a beautiful flavour for use as a fish or mussel soup. The same with vegetables, you cook them one after the other. You are building on flavour. These are the basics of cooking.

Balance is important. Say you are using four flavours in a dish, you have to balance these four flavours. You can only achieve that balance by your experience of those flavours—not a teaspoon of this and a teaspoon of that—but only by tasting and the touch of your finger.

Another example: my mother taught me to cook mushrooms reducing the moisture. Cook them slowly with a whole garlic clove and parsley until all the moisture is gone and you have a concentrated flavour and a crunchy texture. A simple thing, but if you taste my mushrooms, they are beautiful. As I said before—flavour, flavour, flavour. That is the most important thing.

Service. The single most important thing for a waiter

The best food in the world, delivered badly, by a surly waiter, in an inhospitable room, will not taste good and will not induce a customer to return. No-one knows the truth of this more than Beppi Polese. His entire life has been spent delivering the best possible food in the best possible manner to his customers. He learnt his craft in some of the finest hotels and restaurants in Italy, advancing slowly through the ranks by merit (as judged and promoted by his head waiters), and then introducing that knowledge to a new country and adapting it to different circumstances with singular success except, it has to be admitted, in Wagga.

Yet his advice to those who would become good waiters is remarkably simple—and practical.

Below: A family reunion in 1995. From left, Anna (who currently lives 30 km west of Polcenigo), Gigi (who still lives in San Giovanni), Mama Caterina, Beppi and Teresina (who lives near Rome).

Left: Beppi and Norma at their property in Orchard Hills in the mid-1970s.

The service at Beppi's is not, as the acerbic English restaurant critic A A Gill wrote in one review, 'resting while its agent placed the treatment/novel/play'. All of Beppi's all-male waiters are professionals whose day and night job is waiting, and none of them is younger than thirty, and many, like his chefs, have been with him for years. Vito Mariniello and Leo Georgallis began in 1990, and are still there today, as is Giancarlo Sartori, the head waiter who began in 1994. The all-important cashiers were also long servers: Jill Jack from 1978 to 1999, Betty Denham from 1979 to 1993 among them.

The Brisbane food journalist and wit Jan Power once wrote that in the theatre that is a restaurant '... Waiting staff become the lead players and what play is a success if the lead parts are played by less than wonderful actors?'

Male waiters are more suitable for my place. This is not a modern restaurant. I keep telling them, you do better for the business, and you do better for yourself. But remember it's a team which has to work in conjunction with the kitchen. If the food is no good, you can smile until kingdom come and you won't get any sympathy from the customer.

When a waiter comes to work here, no matter how experienced he is, we make him work as a runner—a commis in my language—bringing the dishes and collecting the finished plates. I explain to him why—I say, this place is unique and for you, it's better to learn our way and our dishes while you're running so you know everything before I give you your own section. Some pick it up quickly, some never pick it up.

The way we're set up here, and always have been, with the cashier seated at the front, a customer walks in and there's always someone here to greet them, check their booking and refer them on to the head waiter who comes and takes them to their table. There should be no discomfort at all.

A waiter must be fast, gentle, patient and above all attentive. If he walks through the dining room, it doesn't matter how many plates he is carrying, he must always look at every table, even those that are not his, because there may be people there who need a glass of water or a toothpick or anything. It should not be difficult to get the attention of a waiter if the waiter is attentive. If I'm in the restaurant and talking to someone, I'm also always looking around at the tables—some people think this is rude, but that is how

I've been trained. When I walk through the restaurant, I look at every table as I go. If I see a customer moving, I stop and ask if there is anything they want.

As a waiter, you suggest dishes, you suggest wines, you explain the dishes and explain the flavours, but you must never pressure the customer into a particular dish or push them to buy a more expensive wine. You always allow customers to make up their own mind.

People don't like to be disturbed. Once you say hello, make them welcome, take the order, be gentle. And remember they don't come here to talk to the waiter—if they do want to talk, they must take the first step. For instance, I had an old customer in here today, we have known each other for many years, and we always talk about the past. But you can overdo it. So I say, 'Excuse me, I've got something to attend to'. That is where the waiter has to be perceptive. In this job you learn how to read and approach people.

You have to be dedicated to the job and you have to think about what you're doing. For instance, people come here and they like a beer before their meal and their wine. I say to the waiters, never wait for them to finish the beer before you pour the wine—even white wine—because all wines, even white, need to breathe. If you put the wine in the glass it has contact with oxygen, and by the time they're ready to drink it, it tastes better.

I don't like anything served with the sauce on the plate, always on the side. You give the customer the choice of whether they like it or not—if you put the sauce on the plate they have to eat it and I don't want to impose my will. When I eat out I always ask for the sauces on the side—they look at me like I'm crazy. But it's an example of how we do things a little differently here.

But the worst offence for a waiter is to leave a customer waiting for anything. If you have to wave your arm to attract attention, that's bad.

As a customer, you're sitting down and you're stuck. A good waiter sees everything, and notices if something is missing.

I like the system here in Australia, it's very democratic. In Italy, the system is good, but impersonal. Everything is smooth but you are like a robot. I have taken the best parts of the Italian system, and adapted them to Australia. Here is a different way of treating people. I have ministers of government, owners of newspapers, they are kind, nice. They say, 'Hello Beppi, how are you?' One very important newspaper owner would stand up at the table when I came over to him and introduce me to his guests. Here was the 'in place' to come, but it remained friendly.

Let me tell you a story of bad service. Norma and I have always gone out and eaten at other restaurants. We went to one, I won't mention the name. Now, I have always hated oil since I was a kid. And I had this *carpaccio* and it was swimming in oil. I said to the waiter, 'I can't eat this', and I told him why. And the waiter said, 'This is how we do it'. And I said, 'Well, if that's how you do it, eat it yourself'. So he took it back to the kitchen, and the owner ... he's also the chef ... came out looking very angry—I thought he was going to hit me—then he saw me and he said, 'Aaaah, Beppi, Beppi, Beppi, whatever you want'. Now, if someone says they don't like oil, I'm sorry, we'll do it again. You don't find the owner coming out. How can you scare customers like that? He scared me.

Now when I look back, I realise when I compare how we were when we started off, it took twelve to fourteen years to achieve this style.

Being a host. And always being fantastic

In the 2006 *Good Food Guide*, all but one of the six restaurants receiving that guide's top award of three hats are chef-owned and the one exception, est., has a headlined chef in the kitchen. Down one rung to the two hats, and again all but one of a much longer list (sixteen) are chef-owned.

Beppi's and its sister Mezzaluna, and perhaps three other restaurants in Sydney's upper echelon, are places where the identity of the cook is less important than the personality of the host. And of those, possibly only Beppi Polese could say, as did Claude Terrail of La Tour d'Argent in Paris, in an article by David Dale, 'If I am doing my job properly, there could be different people in the kitchen every night and people would never know'.

Even if there aren't different people in the kitchen every night at Beppi's, it does remain unique in Sydney in not being 'chef-led'. Sydney, in 2006, is chef infatuated.

Beppi Polese is the host. In a practical sense, that means he can—and has—done every job in the restaurant from scrubbing the floors up. But there is more to it than being multi-skilled. The host (or hostess) creates the mood, the personality of the restaurant, is the architect of the feeling you get when you walk in, sit down, and turn yourself over to its theatre, a theatre in which the host is the director, and you, the customer, are part of the cast.

As a host, you must have confidence in the menu, you must have full knowledge of all the dishes so that you can answer any question. You have to have control, but your welcome must be friendly. The idea is to treat the customer gently and with respect.

I'm not a person who goes around to customers and asks them how they liked the food—if I'm not confident, they're not. But it's up to me to look at the dishes and if something is left, to find out that way.

When people ask me how I am, I say—fantastic! They don't want to know my problems. Maybe they want to tell me their problems, and then I have to listen. It is your job as a host to relax the customer and be friendly.

Inclination is important. You have to like what you are doing, and then you will do it naturally. But the basics of the job of host is to know everything about the restaurant. It is very important to understand every job. I could walk into the kitchen, and take over.

I worry when I'm busy. I worry all the time. It doesn't matter how busy we are or how quiet we are. It's what I know and love.

When my sister found me a job in the hotel in Milan at the age of fourteen—after two weeks, I said to myself—this is it. This is the game I want to be in. And I worked so hard! Since 1941, I've probably walked twice around the world doing this job.

Beppilogue

In the early 1990s, prior to establishing his first Cordon Bleu cooking school in the region here, Andre Cointreau said, 'Ten years ago, I thought it was going to be Tokyo. But now, in my opinion, it is Sydney making the kind of synthesis that was made in Paris 100 years ago'.

In 2005, writing in *The Los Angeles Times*, staff writer and usually stingy with praise food critic S Irene Virbila wrote, 'Sydney seems to do practically every kind of food spectacularly well too. So much so that this city of 3 million has become a Mecca of sorts for anyone serious enough about food to get on a plane and fly 15 hours to get here'.

Apart from underestimating our population by one million, she apparently liked what she ate. As did R W (Johnny) Apple, retired Washington correspondent and then roaming food editor for *The New York Times*. 'Having elevated their city into the ranks of the world's great eating towns right up there with NY, Paris and London, chefs here have begun to focus on making the most of the magnificent raw materials at their disposal rather than emphasising the razzle-dazzle of the old.'

Gastronomically, the city has come a long way since Beppi Polese first opened his doors on 11 June 1956. Today, it is as hard to get a really bad meal in Sydney as it was, back then, to get a good one.

And, as has been the case for some time, many of those meals are Italian. Italian remains one of our two, along with Chinese, favourite cuisines. *The Sydney Morning Herald* food critic Simon Thomsen has pronounced 2006 the year of Italian food. 'Probably because you can do very good but affordable food', Thomsen said, 'you can use quality ingredients, treat them simply and they can shine. And it's a reflection of the increasingly prevalent trend to casual dining—a style that was pioneered by the Italians'.

And while it would be stretching it a bit to credit Beppi Polese with this, it should be remembered that Beppi's was the first port of call for so many of the

Beppi and Norma in November 2006.

young Italians who went off to open their own restaurants in Sydney, starting with Aldo Zuzza, who went on to open Darcy's in Paddington with another ex-Beppi's waiter, Attilio Marinangeli. Aldo's younger brother, Beppino opened the The Mixing Pot in Glebe. Giuseppe Mascolo also worked at Beppi's before opening his own restaurant in Leichhardt, Mariu. Armando Percuoco's father Mario worked for Beppi briefly—very briefly—two hours. They did not get on. Armando is now the chef/patron at Buon Ricordo in Paddington. Another young Italian arriving in 1975, Lino Mascolo, Giuseppe's younger brother, worked at Beppi's before opening his own restaurant, Lino's in North Sydney.

The influences cast over the city from this tangled web of familial and professional connections continues. And, at its centre, the figure of Beppi Polese. Any feuds that they all had back in those days are, today, largely forgotten.

What remains is a restaurant and a restaurateur and his partner in life and business who continue to serve the kind of Italian food they began serving back then to an audience who seems never to tire of it. The people of Sydney should be thankful that the young Beppi Polese left his Northern Italian village to try his luck in Sydney.

In September of 2006, Beppi and Norma Polese were given the Lifetime Achiever Award by Restaurant & Catering NSW, their industry association. They stood side by side on the podium to the applause of the 800 restaurateurs in the vast hall. A nervous Beppi (he hates public speaking) hugged Norma and told her he loved her and thanked her for everything.

It was the speech of the night.

Acknowledgments

There's a saying in Italian that Norma and I love, *Chi va piano va sano é lontano* (he that goes slowly, goes healthy and far).

After fifty years in the restaurant there are a lot of people I'd like to thank from along my journey. Firstly, my wife Norma for helping me build the restaurant in the early years and always being there, giving me support. I'd like to thank her and my son, Marc, for their patience and understanding.

I'd also like to thank my parents-in-law for their assistance, and supplying me with lots of different herbs and vegetables I was otherwise unable to find in the early days. Likewise, I'd like to thank my fishmongers from those times, the Crisafi brothers, who provided me with seafood ingredients never tried before in Sydney restaurants.

To all of the staff who have collaborated with me over the years, I'd like to give great thanks—Giuseppe Arena, Marino Gullo, Tony Biondi and Djamel Douadi— chefs that have worked so hard, they have been the backbone of the business, and also their kitchen staff, particularly Maria Rimi. Thank you too, to my waiters and the entire front of house team over the years for their professionalism and skill, and always working together. In my business, all the staff are important and I'd like to thank them all—for their suggestions and their respect.

Finally, I'd like to thank the people who brought this book together. To David Dale for his early work on the project and John Newton for following it through to the end. Thank you very much to Murdoch Books—to Juliet Rogers and Kay Scarlett for giving me the opportunity to share my story and for their trust in it. Thank you to the designer, Reuben Crossman, and the photographer, Alan Benson—magnificent!, and to my editor, Emma Hutchinson, for all her work.

Conversion guide

LIQUID MEASURES

ml	fl oz	volume
5 ml		1 teaspoon
15/20 ml	½ fl oz	
60 ml	2 fl oz	¼ cup
125 ml	4 fl oz	½ cup
185 ml	6 fl oz	¾ cup
250 ml	9 fl oz	1 cup
375 ml	13 fl oz	1½ cups
500 ml	17 fl oz	2 cups
750 ml	26 fl oz	3 cups
1 litre	35 fl oz	4 cups
1.25 litres	44 fl oz	5 cups
1.5 litres	52 fl oz	6 cups

WEIGHT CONVERSIONS

g	oz
5 g	⅛ oz
20 g	¾ oz
50 g	1¾ oz
100 g	3½ oz
150 g	5½ oz
200 g	7 oz
250 g	9 oz
300 g	10½ oz
350 g	12 oz
400 g	14 oz
500 g	1 lb 2 oz
1 kg	2 lb 4 oz

OVEN TEMPERATURES

°C	°F	Gas
100	200	½
120	235	½
140	275	1
160	315	2–3
180	350	4
200	400	6

Published in 2007 by Pier 9, an imprint of Murdoch Books Pty Limited

Murdoch Books Australia
Pier 8/9
23 Hickson Road
Millers Point NSW 2000
Phone: +61 (0)2 8220 2000
Fax: +61 (0)2 8220 2558
www.murdochbooks.com.au

Murdoch Books UK Limited
Erico House, 6th Floor
93–99 Upper Richmond Road
Putney, London SW15 2TG
Phone: +44 (0) 20 8785 5995
Fax: +44 (0) 20 8785 5985

Chief Executive: Juliet Rogers
Publishing Director: Kay Scarlett

Concept and Design: Reuben Crossman
Project Manager and Editor: Emma Hutchinson
Recipe compilation and additional text: David Dale
Food Editor: Leanne Kitchen
Photography, pages 6, 7, 8, 36, 43, 75, 92, 151, 162, 180, 196, 208: Alan Benson
Production: Maiya Levitch

All rights reserved. No part of this publication may be reproduced, stored in a retrieval system or transmitted in any form or by any means, electronic, mechanical photocopying, recording or otherwise without prior permission of the publisher.

National Library of Australia Cataloguing-in-Publication Data
Polese, Beppi.
         Beppi : a life in three courses.

         ISBN 978 1 74045 877 1.

         ISBN 1 74045 877 X.

         1. Polese, Beppi. 2. Beppi's (Restaurant : Sydney, N.S.W.).
         3. Restaurateurs - New South Wales - Sydney - Biography.
         4. Cookery, Italian. I. Newton, John, 1945- . II. Title.

Printed by Midas Printing (Asia) Ltd in 2007. PRINTED IN CHINA.

Text and design copyright © Murdoch Books Pty Limited 2007

All rights reserved. No part of this publication may be reproduced, stored in a retrieval system or transmitted in any form or by any means, electronic, mechanical, photocopying, recording or otherwise, without the prior written permission of the publisher.